S0-AKH-574

Cooking with BC Wine

A guide to the wineries of British Columbia

1st edition – May 2005

Copyright © 2005 by Troy Townsin and Cheryl-Lynn Townsin

Polyglot Publishing
126B St Andrews Street, Victoria, BC, V8V2M7
www.polyglotpublishing.com

Food preparation, styling and photography by Gary Faessler
(exceptions noted)
Cover design by Cassandra Whalen – cwhalen@kutana.com
Edited by Michael Strang – mstrang@kutana.com

Printed and bound in Victoria, BC by Rolex Plastics
www.rolexplastics.com

ISBN 0-9737748-0-0
ISSN 1715-0116

All rights reserved. No part of this publication may be reproduced, stored in a retrieval system or transmitted in any way or by any means, electronic, mechanical, photocopying, recording or otherwise, except brief extracts for the purpose of review, without written permission from the publisher.

HOW CAN WE IMPROVE?

At Polyglot Publishing we strive for excellence in everything that we do. We value any feedback that will help us to make better books and we would love to hear your suggestions. Also, if you come across any information that is out-of-date we appreciate you letting us know so that we can amend future editions of the book. Please feel free to tell us which recipes you like and which ones you do not so we can keep the book chock full of your favourites. Please email us at contactus@polyglotpublishing.com.

Cooking with BC Wine

A guide to the wineries of British Columbia

Troy and Cheryl-Lynn Townsin

Polyglot Publishing

COVER PHOTOGRAPH

Thank you to Quails' Gate Estate Winery for providing us with the magnificent cover photograph taken by photographer Brian Sprout. The photograph was taken at the Old Vines Patio Restaurant at Quails' Gate Estate Winery.

Quails' Gate Estate Winery

Location: 3303 Boucherie Road, Kelowna, BC

Telephone/Fax: (250) 769-4451, 1 (800) 420-9463 / (250) 769-3451

Restaurant: 1 (800) 420-9463 and press #5 for Old Vines Patio.

Website and Email: www.quailsgate.com, info@quailsgate.com

Wine Shop, Tours and Tastings: Wine shop is open year-round, daily except Christmas, Boxing and New Year's Day. Call for hours and tour details.

Getting There: From Kelowna after crossing the floating bridge, turn south (left) off Highway 97 at Boucherie Road. The wine shop is located on the corner of Boucherie and Sunnydale (5 minutes drive from Highway 97).

Highlights: Named 'BC Winery of the Year 2004' by Winepress Northwest. You can dine in style at the Old Vines Patio open May-October

BACK COVER

Photograph of River's Bend Braised Lamb Shanks by Gary Faessler with food preparation by John Waller.

Introduction

This book is a tribute to the British Columbia wine industry. All over the province winemakers are producing world-class wine that is now starting to achieve the international recognition and accolades that it deserves. From the tip of Vancouver Island to the metropolis of Vancouver, by the Shuswap Lakes and down through the deserts of Osoyoos, vineyards are producing wine that delights all those who try it. By creating a combined cookbook and region guide we hope to entice you to undertake a culinary journey with us through the beautiful province that is British Columbia.

This book contains a collection of more than 100 recipes for cooking with wine. Many of the recipes come directly from the numerous wineries located throughout British Columbia. The people who run these wineries have been a wonderful help, providing us with a wealth of information for this book. Some of the recipes they have shared are family secrets that are being published here for the first time. Others are adaptations of old classics and some have been created by world-renowned chefs especially for this book. All of the recipes have been tried and tested by us or by the wineries that supplied them and we are sure you will enjoy them.

Cooking with quality wine is fun. It is also very rewarding and the right wine can make the difference between a good meal and a great meal. The golden rule for cooking with wine is you must *never* cook with a wine that you would not drink. This means you must never use anything called "cooking wine" as these awful concoctions are full of vinegar and salt and can ruin a perfectly good meal.

You may be surprised to learn that cooking with wine has certain health benefits. Not only do studies show that wine is beneficial for the heart, cooking with wine also helps reduce your salt intake by increasing the flavour of the meal. Do your health a favour and include a little wine in your cooking!

Do not worry too much about the alcoholic content of the wine when you are cooking. When wine is heated, the alcohol in the wine is significantly reduced. However, it would require a lot of cooking time to *completely* remove the alcohol. If someone cannot consume *any* alcohol, then it is safer not to serve him or her food cooked with wine. That only leaves more for the rest of us! As you work your way through the recipes in this book you will discover that not only is cooking with wine easy, it is also fun, rewarding and social.

British Columbia is abundant in magnificent fresh produce and we whole-heartedly believe that it is best to use local ingredients when preparing your meals. We have tried to include recipes that cater to as wide a variety of tastes as possible, although it is only fair to warn you that we do love garlic. If you think there is a bit too much garlic in a recipe for your tastes, feel free to tone it down.

Besides being a functional cookbook, this book is also a region guide which lists all of the province's magnificent wineries. We have included maps to make touring easier and more enjoyable. A great addition to the highways of British Columbia has been the distinctive "Wine Route" signs that point out where many of the wineries are located and makes finding them so much easier. So get out there and enjoy British Columbia's spectacular scenery, visit the wineries, grab a corkscrew and a bottle of your favourite wine and use this book to cook yourself up an unforgettable feast.

Best wishes,

Troy and Cheryl-Lynn Townsin

NOTE

New wineries are constantly opening and old wineries are often changing their hours of operation, closing down or changing names, but every effort has been made to include complete and accurate information about every winery in British Columbia. Still, it pays to call in advance of your arrival at a winery to avoid any disappointments.

Table of Contents

"A Celebration of BC Foods and Wine"

by Gary Faessler

British Columbia's wine industry has come a long way since Father Charles Pandosy, an Oblate priest, first made communion wines for his mission overlooking Okanagan Lake. Today, each winery has its own charm, producing wines from vineyards distinct in flavour and character, emulating the individual style and personality of the winemaker.

In the autumn, trees bluster with leaves of red, yellow and saffron and acres of grapevines swell with sweet bunches of jade, inky-blue and magenta fruit. After months of hard work, with vintners carefully nurturing and tending the vines under the hot sun, the grapes have flourished and clusters hang exposed and heavy with juice. When they reach their optimum, usually by the beginning of October, the grapes are handpicked, the flesh crushed and the pressed juice made lovingly into wine.

The Okanagan Valley is British Columbia's principal wine producing area and has the distinction of being the northernmost desert viticultural area in the world. The low rainfall allows wine growers to use irrigation so they can apply just the right amount of water to the vines. This produces small, tasty grapes with concentrated flavours instead of fat, watery ones. The dry climate in the Okanagan also means fewer problems with mildew, fungal diseases and insects, so there is no need to spray the vines with chemicals, pesticides and herbicides. The Okanagan's long, hot autumn days mature and sweeten the grapes, while the dramatic change to cool temperatures at night (this is a desert) promote a slow loss of acidity. It is this combination of high sugar content, good acidity and intense grape varietal character that make wines made in the Okanagan truly unique.

Today in British Columbia we are producing full-bodied, creamy and complex champagne-style wines, internationally celebrated icewines, buttery Chardonnays, crisp Pinot Gris and spicy Gewürztraminer. From the southern area of the Okanagan come stunning reds, albeit in small quantities, like Cabernet Sauvignon, Cabernet Franc, Merlot and Syrah. Distinctive to British Columbia, these reds are fresher, fruitier and cleaner tasting then reds made elsewhere in the world. Yes, we have a lot to celebrate. There are now more than 80 superb wineries throughout the Okanagan Valley, Vancouver Island, Saturna Island, Thetis Island, Salt Spring Island and the Fraser Valley.

Chefs in British Columbia bring to the kitchen a profound respect for ingredients and a growing commitment to use our unique local wines and abundance of regional foods. From the men and women who grow the grapes and make the wine, fish our waters, raise the livestock and harvest the fields come slender, delicate spears of asparagus, fragrant earthy morel mushrooms, Salt Spring Island lamb, fleshy silver salmon and luscious bottles of wine.

Today, it is not unusual to see restaurant chefs at the marketplace carefully handling, smelling and tasting our seasonal offerings, an opulence of sensual riches to seduce the senses and molest the wanting palate. Although each chef has a unique and personal cooking style, the dishes they prepare remain simple and clean, allowing the true flavour of the foods and wine of British Columbia to shine. All for you to enjoy!

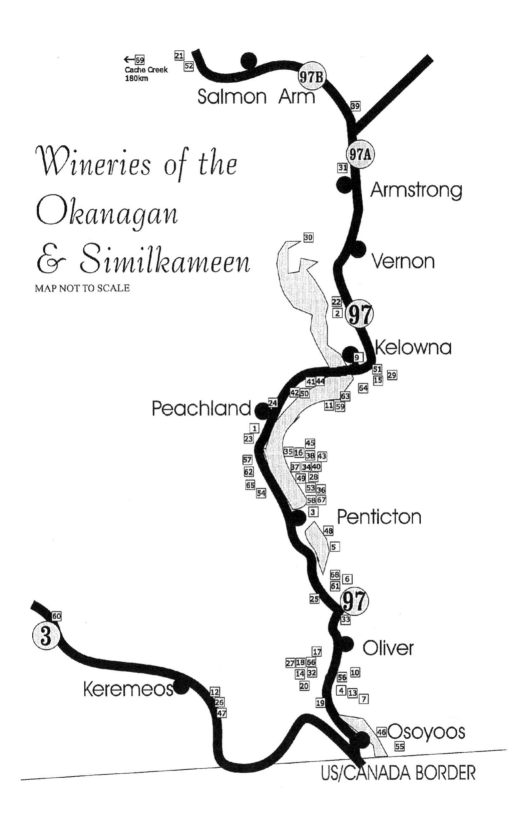

Wineries of the Okanagan & Similkameen

MAP NOT TO SCALE

Wineries of the Okanagan and Similkameen

1 Adora Estate Winery
6807 Highway 97, Summerland
(250) 404-4200
www.adorawines.com
Hours: May 1 – Oct 31, daily 11am – 7pm;
call to confirm.

2 Arrowleaf Cellars
1574 Camp Road, Lake Country
(250) 766-2992
www.arrowleafcellars.com
info@arrowleafcellars.com
Hours: May 1 – Nov 15, daily 10:30am –
5:30pm.

3 Benchland Vineyards
170 Upper Bench Road South, Penticton
(250) 770-1733
www.benchlandwines.com
manager@benchlandwines.com
Hours: May 1 – Oct 31, daily 10am – 6pm;
Nov – Apr, Tues – Fri 2pm – 6pm and Sat –
Sun noon – 6 pm.

4 Black Hills Estate Winery
30880 Black Sage Road, Oliver
(250) 498-0666
www.blackhillswinery.com
info@blackhillswinery.com
Hours: May 1 – May 31, weekends noon –
5pm; Jun 1 – Oct 1, daily noon – 5pm.

5 Blasted Church Vineyards
378 Parsons Road, Okanagan Falls
(250) 497-1125 / 1 (877) 355-2686
www.blastedchurch.com
intrigued@blastedchurch.com
Hours: May – Oct, daily 10am – 5pm.

6 Blue Mountain Vineyard & Cellars
Allendale Road, Okanagan Falls
(250) 497-8244
www.bluemountainwinery.com
bluemountain@bluemountainwinery.com
Hours: By appointment.

7 Burrowing Owl Estate Winery (pg 31)
Black Sage Road, Oliver
(250) 498-0620 / 1 (877) 498-0620
www.burrowingowlwine.ca
info@burrowingowlwine.ca
Hours: Easter - Oct 31, daily 10am - 5pm.

8 Calliope Vinters
Summerland
1 (866) 366-0100 / 1 (250) 494-7213
www.calliopewines.com
sales@calliopewines.com
Hours: No tasting room; call for sales.

9 Calona Vineyards
1125 Richter Street, Kelowna
(250) 762-3332 / 1 (888) 246-4472
www.calonavineyards.ca
requestinfo@calonavineyards.ca
Hours: Summer 9am - 6pm; winter, Mon -
Sat 9am-5pm and Sun 9am-4pm.

10 Carriage House Wines (pg 72)
32764 Black Sage Road, Oliver
(250) 498-8818
www.carriagehousewines.ca
wineinfo@carriagehousewines.ca
Hours: Easter - Nov 11, daily 10am - 6pm;
or by appointment.

11 CedarCreek Estate Winery
5445 Lakeshore Road, Kelowna
(250) 764-8866 / 1 (800) 730-9463
www.cedarcreek.bc.ca
info@cedarcreek.bc.ca
Hours: May - Oct, daily 10am - 6pm; Nov -
Apr, daily 11am - 5pm.

12 Crowsnest Vineyards
Surprise Drive, Cawston
(250) 499-5129
www.crowsnestvineyards.com
info@crowsnestvineyards.com
Hours: May-Oct, daily 10am-6pm; winter
daily 10am-4pm.

13 Desert Hills Estate Winery
30480 Black Sage Road, Oliver
(250) 498-1040
www.deserthills.ca
Hours: Apr 11 - Oct 30, daily 10am - 6pm;
Nov 1 - Mar 30, daily 10am - 5pm.

14 Domaine Combret Estate Winery
32057 #13 Road, Oliver
(250) 498-6966 / 1 (866) 837-7647
www.combretwine.com
info@combretwine.com
Hours: Open all year, 9am-dusk.

15 East Kelowna Cider Company
   2960 McCulloch Road, Kelowna
   (250) 860-8118
   Hours: Call ahead to make an appointment.

16 Elephant Island Orchard Wines
   2730 Aikens Loop, Naramata
   (250) 496-5522
   www.elephantislandwine.com
   info@elephantislandwine.com
   Hours: May 1 - Oct 14, daily 10:30am -
   5:30pm.

17 Fairview Cellars Estate Winery
   13147 334th Avenue, Oliver
   (250) 498-2211
   beggert@img.net
   Hours: Open May - Oct, Tue-Sat 1pm-5pm;
   rest of the year by appointment.

18 Gehringer Brothers Estate Winery
   Number 8 Road at Highway 97, Oliver
   (250) 498-3537 / 1 (800) 784-6304
   Hours: May long weekend - Thanksgiving
   weekend, daily 10am-5pm; rest of the year,
   Mon - Fri 10am-5pm.

19 Gersighel Wineberg
   Highway 97, between Rd 20 & Rd 21, Oliver
   (250) 495-3319
   Hours: Open summer, daily 9:30am-5pm;
   rest of the year by appontment.

20 Golden Mile Cellars
   13140 316A Avenue (Road 13), Oliver
   (250) 498-8330
   www.goldenmilecellars.com
   winery@goldenmilecellars.com
   Hours: May 1 - Oct 31, daily 10am - 6pm.

21 Granite Creek Estate Wines (Pg 88,89)
   2302 Skimikin Road, Tappen
   (250) 835-0049
   www.granitecreek.ca
   Hours: Apr, May, Jun, Oct, daily noon -
   5pm; Jul - Sep, daily 10am - 5pm; Nov 1 -
   Mar 31 by appointment.

22 Gray Monk Estate Winery
   1055 Camp Road, Okanagan Centre
   (250) 766-3168 / 1 (800) 663-4205
   www.graymonk.com
   mailbox@graymonk.com
   Hours: Jul - Aug, daily 9am - 9pm; spring
   and fall, daily 10am - 5pm; winter, 11am -
   5pm. Jan - Mar closed Sundays.

23 Greata Ranch Vineyards
   697 Highway 97 South, Peachland
   (250) 767-2768
   www.cedarcreek.bc.ca/greataranch.htm
   Hours: Open mid-May – mid-Oct, daily
   10am-6pm; Nov, Dec, Mar, Apr, daily
   11am-4pm. Closed Dec – mid-Apr.

**24 Hainle Vineyards and Deep Creek
   Wine Estate (Pg 187)**
   5355 Trepanier Bench Road, Peachland
   (250) 767-2525 / 1 (800) 767-3109
   www.hainle.com
   info@hainle.com
   Hours: Daily 10am - 7pm.

25 Hawthorne Mountain Vineyards
   2575 Green Lake Road, Okanagan Falls
   (250) 497-8267
   www.hmvineyard.com
   info@hmvineyard.com
   Hours: Open Jan-Sep, daily 9am-5pm; Nov-
   Dec, Mon-Fri 9am-5pm and Sat-Sun 11am-
   5pm.

26 Herder Winery & Vineyards (Pg 127)
   716 Lowe Drive, Cawston
   (250) 499-5595
   www.herder.ca
   info@herder.ca
   Hours: May - Oct, daily 10am - 6pm.

27 Hester Creek Estate Winery
   13163 – 326th Avenue, Oliver
   (250) 498-4435
   www.hestercreek.com
   info@hestercreek.com
   Hours: Daily 10am - 5pm.

28 Hillside Estate Winery
   1350 Naramata Road, Penticton
   1 (888) 923-9463
   www.hillsideestate.com
   sales@hillsideestate.com
   Hours: Summer hours: mid-April – mid-Oct,
   daily 9am-5pm. Winter hours: daily noon-
   4pm.

29 House of Rose Winery (Pg 77)
   2270 Garner Road, Kelowna
   (250) 765-0802
   www.winegrowers.bc.ca
   arose@shuswap.net
   Hours: Open every day, except Christmas
   10am-6pm.

30 Hunting Hawk Winery at O'Keefe Ranch
9380 Highway 97, Vernon
(250) 308-6433
www.huntinghawkvineyards.com
hunthawk@cnx.net
Hours: Open May, Jun, Sep and Oct, daily
10am-5pm; Jul, Aug 10am-8pm.

31 Hunting Hawk Vineyards
4758 Gulch Road, Armstrong
(250) 546-2164
www.huntinghawkvineyards.com
hunthawk@cnx.net
Hours: Call ahead for hours.

32 Inniskillin Okanagan Vineyards (Pg 78,79)
Road 11, Oliver
(250) 498-6663 / 1 (800) 498-6211
www.inniskillin.com
info@inniskillin.com
Hours: Open Nov-Apr, Mon-Fri 10am-3pm;
May-Oct, daily 10am-5pm.

33 Jackson-Triggs Vintners
38691 Highway 97 North, Oliver
(250) 498-4961
www.jacksontriggswinery.com
okanaganestate@jacksontriggswinery.com
Hours: Mon - Fri 9am - 4:30pm.

34 Joie Farm Cooking School
2825 Naramata Road, Naramata
1 (866) 422-5643
www.joie.ca
Heidi-Michael@joie.ca
No tasting room at present. Call for sales.

35 Kettle Valley Winery
2988 Hayman Road, Naramata
(250) 496-5898
www.kettlevalleywinery.com
info@kettlevalleywinery.com
Hours: May - Oct, daily 11am - 5pm; or by
appointment.

36 La Frenz Winery (Pg 108)
740 Naramata Road, Penticton
(250) 492-6690
www.lafrenzwinery.com
lafrenz@shaw.ca
Hours: Mid-May - Oct, daily 10am - 5pm; or
by appointment.

37 Lake Breeze Vineyards
930 Sammet Road, Naramata
(250) 496-5659
www.lakebreezewinery.ca
lakebreeze@telus.net
Hours: Daily May-Oct, call for hours.

38 Lang Vineyards
2493 Gammon Road, Naramata
(250) 496-5987
www.langvineyards.com
langvineyards@shaw.ca
Hours: May - Oct, daily 10am - 5pm; or by
appointment.

39 Larch Hills Estate Winery (Pg 66)
110 Timms Road, Salmon Arm
(250) 832-0155
www.larchhillswinery.com
info@larchhillswinery.com
Hours: Apr 1 - Oct 31, daily noon - 5pm.

40 Laughing Stock Vineyards (Pg 114)
1548 Naramata Road, Penticton
(250) 493-8466
www.laughingstock.ca
info@laughingstock.ca
Hours: Opening Fall 2005. Call ahead to
confirm hours.

41 Little Straw Vineyards (Pg 26)
2815 Ourtoland Road, Kelowna
(250) 769-0404
www.littlestraw.bc.ca
info@littlestraw.bc.ca
Hours: Apr - Oct, daily 10am - 5:30pm.

42 Mission Hill Family Estate (Pg 174, 175)
1730 Mission Hill Road, Westbank
(250) 768-7611
www.missionhillwinery.com
info@missionhillwinery.com
Hours: Weekdays 10am-5pm and weekends
10am-6pm, except Christmas, Boxing and
New Year's Day. Extended summer hours.

43 Mistral Estate Winery
250 Upper Bench Road, Penticton
(250) 770-1733
www.mistralestatewinery.com
manager@mistralestatewinery.com
Hours: Hours of operation not yet confirmed
call ahead for details.

44 Mt. Boucherie Estate Winery (Pg 92)
829 Douglas Road, Kelowna
(250) 769-8803 / 1 (877) 684-2748
www.mtboucherie.bc.ca
sales@mtboucherie.bc.ca
Hours: Daily 10am - 6pm in summer; 11am
- 5pm in winter.

45 Nichol Vineyard (Pg 124)
1285 Smethurst Road, Naramata
(250) 496-5962
www.nicholvineyard.com
nicholvineyard@shaw.ca
Hours: Late Jun - Thanksgiving, Tue - Sun
11am - 5pm. Also open Easter weekend,
Okanagan Spring Wine Festival and May
long weekend.

46 Nk'Mip Cellars (Pg 35)
1400 Rancher Creek Road, Osoyoos
(250) 495-2985
www.nkmipcellars.com
winery@nkmip.ca
Hours: Open summer, daily 9am-7pm;
winter, daily 10am-4pm; spring and fall
9am-5pm. Call to confirm.

47 Orofino Vineyards
2152 Barcello Road, Cawston
(250) 499-0068
orofino@nethop.net
Hours: Summer hours 10am-5pm. Rest of
the year by appointment.

48 Pentâge Winery (Pg 40)
4400 Lakeside Road, Penticton
(250) 493-4008
www.pentage.com
pentage@vip.net
Hours: By appointment.

49 Poplar Grove Winery (Pg 103)
1060 Poplar Grove Road, Penticton
(250) 492-4575
www.poplargrove.ca
wine@poplargrove.ca
Hours: Summer hours 11am-5pm;
otherwise by appointment.

50 Quails' Gate Estate Winery (Pg 4)
3303 Boucherie Road, Kelowna
(250) 769-4451 / 1 (800) 420-9463
www.quailsgate.com
info@quailsgate.com
Hours: Daily, except Christmas, Boxing and
New Year's Day. Call for hours.

51 Raven Ridge Cidery Inc. (Pg 169)
3002 Dunster Road, Kelowna
(250) 763-1091
www.k-l-o.com
klo@k-l-o.com
Hours: May 1 - Oct 31, daily 8am-5pm. Call
for winter hours.

52 Recline Ridge Vineyards & Winery (Pg 58)
2640 Skimikin Road, Tappen
(250) 835-2212
www.recline-ridge.bc.ca
inquiry@recline-ridge.bc.ca
Hours: Daily Apr - Jun & Oct, noon - 5pm;
Jul – Sep, 10am - 5pm; or by appointment.

53 Red Rooster Winery (Pg 134)
891 Naramata Road, Penticton
(250) 492-2424
www.redroosterwinery.com
redroosterwinery@shaw.ca
Hours: Apr - Oct, daily 10am - 6pm. Call to
confirm winter hours.

54 Scherzinger Vineyards
7311 Fiske Street, Summerland
(250) 494-8815
www.scherzingervineyards.com
info@scherzingervineyards.com
Hours: Apr 1 - Oct 31, daily 10am -
5:30pm; or by appointment.

55 Seven Stones Winery
1143 Highway 3, Cawston
(250) 499-2144
Hours: Wine shop will open 2006.

56 Silver Sage Winery
32032 – 87th Avenue, Oliver
(250) 498-0310
www.silversagewinery.com
Hours: Open daily 10am-6pm.

57 Sonoran Estate Winery
21606 Highway 97 North, Summerland
(250) 494-9323
www.sonoranestate.com
mail@sonoranestate.com
Hours: Apr – Oct 31, daily 10am - 5:30pm.

58 Spiller Estate Winery
475 Upper Bench Road North, Penticton
(250) 490-4162
www.spillerestates.com
manager@spillerestates.com
Hours: Open Apr 30 - Jun 26, weekends
only 11am-5pm; Jul - Oct 16, daily 11am-
5pm, call ahead to confirm.

59 St. Hubertus Estate Winery (pg 120)
5225 Lakeshore Road, Kelowna
(250) 764-7888
www.st-hubertus.bc.ca
wine@st-hubertus.bc.ca
Hours: Summer, daily 10am - 5:30pm;
winter, Tue - Sat noon - 5pm.

60 St. Laszlo Vineyards
Highway 3, Keremeos
(250) 499-2856
Hours: Daily 9am - 9pm.

61 Stag's Hollow Winery
2237 Sun Valley Way, Okanagan Falls
(250) 497-6162 / 1 (877) 746-5569
www.stagshollowwinery.com
info@stagshollowwinery.com
Hours: Okanagan Spring Wine Festival to
Fall Wine Festival, daily 11am - 4:30pm.

62 Sumac Ridge Estate Winery
17403 Highway 97 North, Summerland
(250) 494-0451
www.sumacridge.com
info@sumacridge.com
Hours: Summer, daily 9am - 9pm. Call to
confirm winter hours.

63 Summerhill Pyramid Winery (Pg 74, 75)
4870 Chute Lake Road, Kelowna
(250) 764-8000 / 1 (800) 667-3538
www.summerhill.bc.ca
info@summerhill.bc.ca
Hours: Open year round, daily 9am-9pm.

64 Tantalus Vineyards
1670 DeHart Road, Kelowna
(250) 764-0078
www.focuswines.com
Hours: Currently no tasting room. Sales by
phone or email. Call for updates.

65 Thornhaven Estates Winery
6816 Andrew Avenue, Summerland
(250) 494-7778
www.thornhaven.com
info@thornhaven.com
Hours: May-Oct, daily 10am-5pm; or by
appointment.

66 Tinhorn Creek Vineyards
32830 Tinhorn Creek Road, Oliver
(250) 498-3743 / 1 (888) 484-4676
www.tinhorn.com
winery@tinhorn.com
Hours: May - mid-Oct, daily 10am - 6pm;
mid-Oct - Apr, daily 10am - 5pm, except
Christmas, Boxing and New Year's Day.

67 Township 7 Okanagan Winery (Pg 135)
1450 McMillan Avenue, Penticton
(250) 770-1743
www.township7.com
wine@township7.com
Hours: Mid-May – mid-Oct; call for details.

68 Wild Goose Vineyards
2145 Sun Valley Way, Okanagan Falls
(250) 497-8919
www.wildgoosewinery.com
roland@wildgoosewinery.com
Hours: Apr 1 - Oct 31, daily 10am - 5pm; or
by appointment

THOMPSON NICOLA

69 Bonaparte Bend Winery (Pg 171)
2520 Cariboo Highway, Cache Creek
(250) 457-6667
www.bbwinery.com
bbwines@coppervalley.com
Hours: Apr-Sep, Mon-Sat 10am-5pm;
Sundays and holidays 10am-4pm.

Wineries of Vancouver & The Fraser Valley

MAP NOT TO SCALE

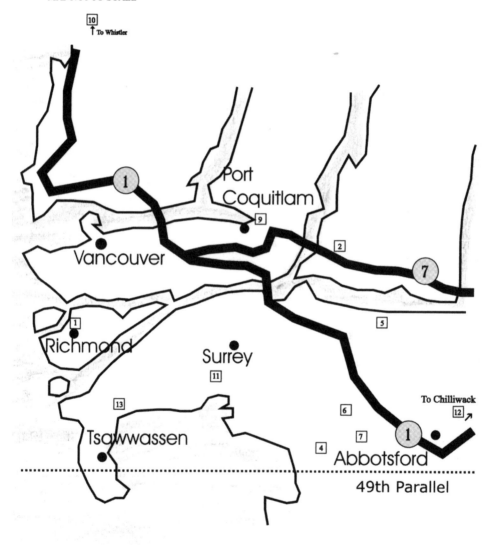

49th Parallel

Wineries of Vancouver and the Fraser Valley

1 BLOSSOM WINERY (Pg 85, 181)
5491 Minoru Boulevard, Richmond
(604) 232-9839
www.blossomwinery.com
info@blossomwinery.com
Hours: Mon - Fri 10am - 6pm and
Sat 11am - 6pm.

2 BLUE HERON FRUIT WINERY
18539 Dewdney Trunk Road, Pitt Meadows
(604) 465-5563
www.blueheronwinery.ca
info@blueheronwinery.ca
Hours: Sun - Thu 10am - 8pm; Fri - Sat
10am - 9pm.

3 D'ASOLO VINEYARDS
Vancouver
(604) 871-4329
www.asolo.ca
info@asolo.ca
Hours: Not open for tours at time of
publication. Check website for updates.

4 DOMAINE DE CHABERTON (Pg 105)
1064-216th Street, Langley
(604) 530-1736 / 1 (888) 332-9463
www.domainedechaberton.com
info@domainedechaberton.com
Hours: Mon - Sat 10am - 6pm; Sun 11am -
6pm.

5 THE FORT WINE COMPANY
26151-84th Avenue, Fort Langley
(604) 857-1101 / 1 (866) 921-9463
www.thefortwineco.com
contact@thefortwineco.com
Hours: Daily 10am - 6pm, except
Christmas, Boxing and New Year's Day.

6 GLENUGIE WINERY (Pg 182)
3033-232nd Street, Langley
(604) 539-9463 / 1 (866) 233-9463
www.glenugiewinery.com
info@glenugiewinery.com
Hours: Sun - Wed noon - 6pm; Thu - Sat
11am - 6pm.

7 LOTUSLAND VINEYARDS (Pg 162)
28450 King Road, Abbotsford
(604) 857-4188
www.lotuslandvineyards.com
info@lotuslandvineyards.com
Hours: Apr - Sep, Wed - Mon 11am - 6pm;
Oct - Mar, Thu - Sun 11am - 5pm; or by
happenchance.

**8 PARADISE RANCH WINES CORP
(Pg 197)**
Vancouver
(604) 683-6040
www.icewines.com
info@icewines.com
Hours: Not a tourable winery.

9 PELLER ESTATES (Pg 152)
2120 Vintner Street, Port Moody
(604) 937-3411
www.andreswines.com
Hours: Open year-round, Mon-Fri 8am-
4pm.

**10 PEMBERTON VALLEY VINEYARD & INN
(Pg 126)**
1427 Collins Road, Pemberton
1 (877) 444-5857
www.whistlerwine.com
bradner@whistlerwine.com
Hours: Open by appointment.

11 RIVER'S BEND WINERY (Pg 116, 117)
15560 Colebrook Road, Surrey
(604) 574-6106
www.riversbendwinery.com
gfaessler@shaw.ca
Hours: Tue-Sun 11am-6pm. Opens early
Summer 2005.

12 ST URBAN WINERY
47189 Bailey Road, Chilliwack
(604) 824-6233
Hours: Plans to open Summer 2005; call for
details.

13 WELLBROOK WINERY (Pg 170)
4626 88th Street, Delta
(604) 946-1868
www.wellbrookwinery.com
Hours: Open daily 11am-6pm

**14 TOWNSHIP 7 VINEYARDS & WINERY
(Pg 135)** (Not shown on map; just
northwest of number 4)
21152 16th Avenue, Langley
(604) 532-1766
www.township7.com
wine@township7.com
Hours: Jan by appointment, Feb-Jun and
Sep-Nov, Thu-Sun. July, Aug, Dec, open
daily 11am-6pm.

Wineries of Vancouver Island & Gulf Islands

16 To Quadra Island
18 To Hornby Island
5 To Port Alberni

6

19 Nanaimo

MAP NOT TO SCALE

Strait of Georgia

Thetis Is.
22

Ladysmith

Cowichan Lake
13

Salt Spring Is.
19

Saturna Is.

1
2
20
10
21

Duncan
27
9 12 3 24
11 8 7
17

4

Pender Is.

Sidney

1

15
28 26
25

14

17

23 14
Sooke

Victoria

Wineries of Vancouver Island and the Gulf Islands

1 ALDERLEA VINEYARDS
1751 Stamps Road, Duncan
(250) 746-7122
Hours: Hours vary; call ahead to make an appointment.

2 AVERILL CREEK VINEYARDS
6552 North Road, Duncan
(250) 715-7379
www.averillcreek.ca
admin@averillcreek.ca
Hours: Opening Sep 2005; call for hours.

3 BLUE GROUSE VINEYARDS (Pg 70)
4365 Blue Grouse Road, Duncan
(250) 743-3834
www.bluegrousevineyards.com
info@bluegrousevineyards.com
Hours: Apr - Sep, Wed - Sun 11am - 5pm;
Oct - Mar, Wed - Sat 11am - 5pm.

4 CHALET ESTATE VINEYARD (Pg 109)
11195 Chalet Road, North Saanich
(250) 656-2552
www.chaletestatevineyard.ca
chaletestate@shaw.ca
Hours: Tue - Sun 11am - 5pm; or by appointment.

5 CHASE & WARREN ESTATE WINES
6253 Drinkwater Road, Port Alberni
(250) 724-4906
Hours: Hours vary; call ahead to make an appointment.

6 CHATEAU WOLFF
2534 Maxey Road, Nanaimo
(250) 753-9669
Hours: Sat-Sun 11am - 5pm

7 CHERRY POINT VINEYARDS (Pg 185)
840 Cherry Point Road, Cobble Hill
(250) 743-1272
www.cherrypointvineyards.com
info@cherrypointvineyards.com
Hours: Daily 10am - 5pm

8 DIVINO ESTATE WINERY
1500 Freeman Road, Cobble Hill
(250) 743-2311
divinowinery@aol.com
Hours: Fri-Sat 1pm - 5pm; or by appointment.

9 ECHO VALLEY VINEYARDS
4651 Waters Road, Duncan
(250) 748-1470
www.echovalley-vineyards.com
chroma@islandnet.com
Hours: Summer, Thu - Sun 1pm - 5pm;
shoulder season, Sat - Sun 1pm - 5pm;
winter by appointment.

10 GARRY OAKS WINERY (Pg 131)
1880 Fulford-Ganges Road, Salt Spring Island
(250) 653-4687
www.garryoakswinery.com
info@garryoakswinery.com
Hours: May - Thanksgiving; or by appointment. Call or email for current hours.

11 GLENTERRA VINEYARDS (Pg 61)
3897 Cobble Hill Road, Cobble Hill
(250) 743-2330
glenterravineyards@shaw.ca
Hours: Mar - Oct, daily 11am - 6pm;
winter, noon - 5pm; or by chance.

12 GODFREY-BROWNELL VINEYARDS
4911 Marshall Road, Duncan
(250) 715-0504
www.gbvineyards.com
info@gbvineyards.com
Hours: Call ahead to confirm hours.

13 HONEYMOON BAY WILD BLACKBERRY WINERY
9940 South Shore Road, Honeymoon Bay
(250) 749-6094
raymogg@telus.net
Hours: Open evenings and weekends; call ahead to confirm hours.

14 MALAHAT ESTATE VINEYARD
1197 Aspen Road, Malahat
(250) 474-5129
Hours: Call ahead to confirm hours.

15 MARLEY FARM WINERY
1831D Mount Newton Crossroads, Saanichton
(250) 652-8667
www.marleyfarm.ca
info@marleyfarm.ca
Hours: Summer, daily 11am - 6pm; Oct - Dec & Mar - May, Wed - Sun noon - 4pm;
Jan - Feb, Sat only noon - 4pm.

16 MARSHWOOD ESTATE WINERY
  548 Jade Road, Heriot Bay, Quadra Island
  (250) 285-2068
  marshwd@connected.bc.ca
  Hours: Call ahead to confirm hours.

17 MERRIDALE CIDERWORKS (Pg 189)
  1230 Merridale Road, Cobble Hill
  (250) 743-4293 / 1 (800) 998-9908
  www.merridalecider.com
  info@merridalecider.com
  Hours: Daily 10:30am - 5:30pm; open until
  7pm on weekends during the summer.

18 MIDDLE MOUNTAIN MEAD (Pg 82)
  3505 Euston Road, Hornby Island
  (250) 335-1392
  www.middlemountainmead.com
  info@middlemountainmead.com
  Hours: Summer, Wed – Sat 1pm-5pm; or
  by appointment. Check website for current
  hours.

19 MORNING BAY FARM
  6621 Harbour Hill Road, Pender Island
  (250) 629-8351
  mrngby@netscape.net
  Hours: Call ahead to confirm hours.

20 SALT SPRING VINEYARDS (Pg 101)
  151 Lee Road, Salt Spring Island
  (250) 653-9463
  www.saltspringvineyards.com
  vineyards@saltspring.com
  Hours: May - Sep, daily noon - 5pm; Feb,
  Mar, Apr, Oct, Dec, Sat noon - 5pm.

21 SATURNA ISLAND VINEYARDS
  8 Quarry Road, Saturna Island
  (250) 539-5139 / 1 (877) 918-3388
  www.saturnavineyards.com
  wine@saturnavineyards.com
  Hours: May - Sep, daily 11:30am - 4:30pm;
  Oct, weekends 11:30am - 4:30pm; or by
  appointment.

22 THETIS ISLAND VINEYARDS
  Clam Bay Road, Thetis Island
  (250) 246-2258
  www.cedar-beach.com
  csparkes@uniserve.com
  Hours: Tue-Sun, 9:30am - noon and 2pm -
  6pm; call ahead to confirm hours.

23 TUGWELL CREEK HONEY FARM & MEADERY
  8750 West Coast Road, Sooke
  (250) 642-1956
  www.tugwellcreekfarm.com
  dana-l@shaw.ca
  Hours: May 1 - Oct 1, Wed - Sun noon -
  5pm; Oct 2 - Apr 31, Sat - Sun noon - 5pm;
  closed Jan.

24 VENTURI-SCHULZE VINEYARDS
  4235 Trans-Canada Highway, Cobble Hill
  (250) 743-5630
  www.venturischulze.com
  Hours: By appointment only.

25 CHURCH & STATE WINES (Pg 52, 53)
  1445 Benvenuto Avenue, Brentwood Bay
  (250) 652-2671
  www.churchandstatewines.com
  Hours: Call ahead to confirm hours.

26 VIGNETI ZANATTA WINERY & VINEYARDS
  5039 Marshall Road, Duncan
  (250) 748-2338
  www.zanatta.ca
  zanatta@zanatta.ca
  Hours: Call ahead to confirm.

27 WINCHESTER CELLARS
  6170 Old West Saanich Road, Victoria
  (250) 544-8218
  Hours: Opening May 2005; call ahead to
  confirm hours

Driving Distances (Approximate)

Calgary – Kelowna: 610km, 7 hrs
Kelowna – Armstrong: 80 km, 1hr 15 min
Kelowna – Osoyoos: 130km, 1 hr 40 min
Kelowna – Penticton: 70km, 1 hr
Kelowna – Vancouver: 400km, 4 hrs 15 min
Osoyoos – Penticton: 55km, 45 min
Osoyoos – Salmon Arm: 230km, 3 hrs
Penticton – Oliver: 45 km, 45 minutes
Salmon Arm – Cache Creek: 190km, 2 hrs 30 min
Salmon Arm – Kelowna: 115km, 1 hr 45 min
Vancouver – Cache Creek: 345km, 4 hrs 15 min
Vancouver – Pemberton: 160km, 2hrs 45 min
Vancouver – Victoria: 110km, 3 hrs (includes ferry)
Victoria – Duncan: 60km, 50 min
Victoria – Nanaimo: 110 km, 2 hrs

Cooking Terms Used in this Book

Al dente – An Italian term to describe a degree of doneness for pasta, rice or vegetables. Al dente pasta should have a slight resistance when you bite into it. Literally means "to the tooth".

All'onda – Another Italian term used to describe rice with a smooth moist consistency that has been prepared for risotto. Literally means "to the wave".

Bain Marie – This is a shallow water bath. Also called a double boiler,. it is used to gently heat delicate foods so that they do not burn. The dish containing the food is placed inside the Bain Marie, which is filled with hot water.

Bouquet Garni – This is a small bunch of herbs tied together or wrapped in cheesecloth. For further information see page 63.

Deglaze – After food has been fried, liquid (usually wine) is added to loosen and dissolve the drippings that have formed during cooking, resulting in a delicious sauce. For a further explanation see page 164.

Double Boiler – Very similar to a Bain Marie, this usually consists of two saucepans with one inside the other. The larger saucepan contains hot water and the smaller contains the food to be heated, usually sauces, chocolate or custard.

Dutch Oven – A heavy cooking pot, usually made of cast iron or enamel on iron. It has a heavy cover and can be used on the stovetop or in the oven.

Julienne – To cut into thin, long strips. This is a term usually used for vegetables, but it can also be applied to meat or fish.

Roux – This is a mixture of butter and flour. It is commonly used for thickening sauces.

Sabayon – A sweet egg yolk dessert or sauce that is flavoured with wine and whisked over gentle heat. In Italy it is called zabaglione.

Easy to Use Cooking Conversion Charts (Approximate)

IMPERIAL	METRIC
¼ tsp	1 ml
½ tsp	2 ml
1 tsp	5 ml
2 tsp	10ml
1 tbsp	15 ml
2 tbsp	25 ml
¼ cup	50 ml
$^1/_3$ cup	75 ml
½ cup	125 ml
$^2/_3$ cup	150 ml
¾ cup	175 ml
1 cup	250 ml

IMPERIAL OZ	IMPERIAL LBS	METRIC
¼ oz	-	7 gm
½ oz	-	15 gm
1 oz	-	30 gm
2 oz	-	55 gm
4 oz	¼ lb	110 gm
5 oz	-	140 gm
8 oz	½ lb	230 gm
10 oz	-	280 gm
16 oz	1 lb	450 gm
24 oz	1½ lbs	680 gm
32 oz	2 lbs	900 gm

Fahrenheit	Celsius
175	80
200	95
225	110
250	120
275	140
300	150
325	160
350	180
375	190
400	200
425	220
450	230

Cooking with BC Wine

Appetizers

I love cooking with wine. Sometimes I even put a little in the food.

Anonymous

Little Straw's Scallops with Leek Sauce

Poached Eggs with a Red Wine Sauce

Steamed Chardonnay Mussels

Sonora Room at Burrowing Owl Goat Cheese and Mission Fig Phyllo Purse

Whole Artichokes in White Wine

Oysters with a Sparkling Wine Sauce

Baked Olives in Red Wine

Nk'Mip Steamed Clams

Baked Crab and Artichoke Dip

Cheesy Spinach and Wine Dip

Cheese Crostini

Pentâge Coquilles St Jacques

Thai Fishcakes with Sweet Chilli Dipping Sauce

Little Straw's Scallops with Leek Sauce

Featuring Little Straw Vineyards Sauvignon Blanc

The 2004 Sauvignon Blanc is a blend of fruit from two different sections of our vineyard. One is from our older plot, which is slightly shaded from the sun; it expresses the asparagus herbal characteristics. The other is a site that gets maximum sunlight and expresses the ripe tropical flavours. The resulting wine has some residual sugar tempered with a good acid finish. This wine was bottled in the spring of 2004, making 300 cases.

Serves 4

INGREDIENTS

$^2/_3$ cup **Little Straw Vineyards Sauvignon Blanc**

2 tbsp olive oil

2 leeks, chopped

1 large cucumber

½ lime, juiced

3 tbsp butter

3 tbsp flat leaf parsley, chopped

16 medium sized scallops

salt and pepper to taste

1. Heat 1 tbsp of olive oil in a frying pan over medium heat. Add chopped leeks and sauté until soft. While leeks are sautéing, halve the cucumber lengthways and remove the seeds with a spoon. Grate the cucumber into a small bowl and strain well, reserving the liquid.

2. Add the **Little Straw Vineyards Sauvignon Blanc** to the pan to deglaze. Add the cucumber juice and the juice from the lime. Reduce the liquid over moderate heat. Add butter to the reduction to thicken the sauce. Adjust to taste with salt and pepper. Reduce heat and stir in 2 tbsp of parsley.

3. In a separate pan, heat remaining olive oil over high heat. Sauté the scallops until browned on both sides. Serve the scallops, placing 4 on each plate. Pour leek sauce over them and garnish with some parsley. Enjoy with a glass of **Little Straw Vineyards Sauvignon Blanc**.

Little Straw Vineyards

Location: 2815 Ourtoland Road, Kelowna, BC

Telephone/Fax: (250) 769-0404 / (250) 763-8168

Website: www.littlestraw.bc.ca

Wine Shop, Tours and Tastings: Wine shop is open Apr – Oct, daily 10am-5:30pm. Tours by appointment.

Getting There: Follow the "Wine Route" signs on the west side of the Okanagan Lake Bridge to Boucherie Road. Then turn away from the lake onto Ogden Road and then turn north on Ourtoland Road.

Highlights: Visit the brand new facility and enjoy current releases in the spacious wine shop overlooking the beautiful Okanagan Valley.

Sauvignon Blanc

PRONOUNCED (SO-VIN-YAWN-BLAHN)

WINE HISTORIANS AGREE THAT THE LOIRE RIVER VALLEY AREA IN FRANCE IS THE HOME OF SAUVIGNON BLANC. THE GRAPE HAS A LONG HISTORY IN THIS REGION AND MANY WINE LOVERS FEEL THAT THESE WINES SET A BENCHMARK FOR ALL COUNTRIES PRODUCING SAUVIGNON BLANC WINES TO ASPIRE TO.

SAUVIGNON BLANC IS ALSO WIDELY KNOWN AS FUMÉ BLANC, A SUCCESSFUL MARKETING TERM COINED BY ROBERT MONDAVI OF CALIFORNIA'S ROBERT MONDAVI WINERY. THIS VARIETY GROWS IN MANY UNLIKELY PLACES AROUND THE WORLD, INCLUDING ISRAEL AND TEXAS. HOWEVER, THERE ARE FEW PLACES THAT HAVE A CLIMATE AS WELL-SUITED TO THE VARIETY AS BRITISH COLUMBIA IN A COOL YEAR. SOME TRULY MAGNIFICENT EXAMPLES OF THIS WINE ARE PRODUCED IN THIS PROVINCE.

THE GRAPE WAS FIRST GROWN IN BRITISH COLUMBIA DURING THE LATE 1970S BUT IT WAS WIPED OUT DURING THE 80S. IT MADE A WELCOME REAPPEARANCE DURING THE 1990S AND FORTUNATELY IT HAS SINCE STAYED WITH US.

THIS WINE IS WELL-KNOWN FOR ITS HERBACEOUS CHARACTERISTICS AND OFTEN HAS GRASSY AROMAS. OTHER FLAVOURS THAT COME THROUGH INCLUDE CITRUS, PASSION FRUIT, FIGS, MELONS AND EVEN BANANA. SOME GREAT FOOD PAIRINGS INCLUDE ANY TYPE OF SEAFOOD, CHICKEN, PORK, GOAT CHEESE, SALADS AND DISHES THAT USE RED PEPPERS.

Poached Eggs with a Red Wine Sauce

Featuring BC Red Wine

Poached eggs as an appetizer! Eggs are not just for breakfast and this is not exactly your usual egg on toast. This wonderful dish is popular in France, where it is occasionally served as a main course.

Serves 6

INGREDIENTS

2 cups **BC Red Wine**

¼ lb bacon, sliced into thin strips

2 tbsp butter

1 tbsp vegetable oil

1 medium onion, chopped

1 large carrot, finely chopped

3 whole garlic cloves, slightly pressed

1 tbsp flour

1 bay leaf

2 cups chicken stock

¼ cup white vinegar

6 eggs

6 thick slices of bread, fried in butter

salt and pepper to taste

1 cup flat leaf parsley, chopped, for garnish

1. Cook bacon in a large pan over medium heat. Set bacon aside when done. Remove excess fat and then heat oil and 1 tbsp of butter in the pan. When the oil is hot, add onion and sauté for 5-6 minutes until soft.

2. Add carrots and garlic to the pan and cook for 5 minutes before adding flour. Stir well and cook for another 3-4 minutes. Return the bacon to the pan and add bay leaf. Pour in the **BC Red Wine** and stock and then increase the heat to bring to a boil. As soon as the sauce boils, reduce heat and simmer for 15-25 minutes, allowing the liquid to reduce to a sauce-like consistency.

3. Remove the bay leaf and garlic. Add remaining butter and stir. Add salt and pepper to taste.

4. In a separate pan, bring 4 cups of water and vinegar to a boil. Give the water a stir to create a whirlpool effect. Crack the eggs one by one into the water. Each egg should take 2-3 minutes to cook. When cooked, remove eggs and place on paper towels to dry.

5. Spoon the sauce into soup bowls and place the fried bread on top of the sauce. Put an egg on each piece of toast. Season with salt and pepper and garnish with chopped parsley. Serve immediately.

Steamed Chardonnay Mussels

Featuring BC Chardonnay

There is evidence that mussels, or moules as they are known in many parts of the world, have been served in gourmet feasts since the time of the Pharaohs in ancient Egypt. This is a simple dish that is guaranteed to please. If you do not want to include the cream in this dish, leave it out. The results will still be wonderful.

Serves 4-5

INGREDIENTS

½ cup **BC Chardonnay**

1 tbsp butter

½ small onion, chopped

1 garlic clove, chopped

40 fresh mussels, beards removed

*see pg 86 for chef's tip on mussels

½ cup cream

½ lemon, juiced

1 small bunch flat leaf parsley, chopped

salt and pepper to taste

crusty bread

1. Melt the butter in a saucepan over medium-high heat. Sweat the onions and garlic until they become translucent, about 4-5 minutes.

2. Add the mussels and then pour in the **BC Chardonnay**. Stir once and cover so that mussels will steam. Leave covered for 2-3 minutes until they have all opened. Discard any mussels that do not open. Transfer mussels to individual serving bowls.

3. Add cream to the sauce along with lemon juice, salt and pepper to taste. Allow mixture to reduce until it becomes slightly thicker.

4. Remove the sauce from the heat and stir in fresh parsley. Pour sauce over the mussels and serve with a wedge of crusty bread for mopping up leftover sauce. Enjoy with a glass of **BC Chardonnay**.

Chardonnay

PRONOUNCED (SHAR-DOE-NAY)

CHARDONNAY IS PROBABLY STILL THE WORLD'S HIPPEST GRAPE. THIS IS THE GRAPE THAT WINEMAKERS IN FRANCE TURN INTO THE FAMOUS WHITE BURGUNDY WINES. MANY BELIEVE THAT THE ARTISTRY OF THE WINEMAKER IS MOST APPARENT IN CHARDONNAY. ITS ORIGINS CAN BE TRACED BACK TO BURGUNDY'S CÔTE D'OR. THE GRAPE HAS BEEN A POPULAR CHOICE OF GROWERS IN BRITISH COLUMBIA SINCE THE LATE 1980S, BUT IT REALLY GAINED POPULARITY DURING THE 1990S.

CHARDONNAY IS OFTEN AGED IN OAK BARRELS, WHICH CAN GIVE THE WINE OVERTONES OF VANILLA OR BUTTERY TOAST. IN THE 1990S, SOME WINERIES STARTED PRODUCING UNOAKED CHARDONNAY AND THE TREND HAS REALLY TAKEN OFF. AS AN EXPERIMENT, TRY AN UNOAKED CHARDONNAY AND THEN AN OAKED CHARDONNAY TO DISCOVER WHAT EFFECT THE OAK HAS HAD ON THE FLAVOUR. CHARDONNAY CAN BE AGED IN THE BOTTLE, ALTHOUGH IT WILL NOT LAST AS LONG AS MOST RED WINES.

CHARDONNAY IS ALMOST ALWAYS DRY. IT CAN CONTAIN DIVERSE FLAVOURS, FROM CITRUS TO APPLES; EVEN FIGS AND PINEAPPLE ARE NOT UNCOMMON FLAVOURS. SOME WONDERFUL PAIRINGS FOR CHARDONNAY INCLUDE FISH, MUSSELS, LOBSTER, CRAB, CHICKEN AND PORK.

Sonora Room at Burrowing Owl Goat Cheese & Mission Fig Phyllo Purse

Featuring Burrowing Owl Pinot Gris

Executive Chef Dominique Couton has developed this intriguing combination of flavours that seems to suit those seeking a leisurely patio lunch at the winery, which overlooks lush vineyards and Osoyoos Lake. One of the most popular wines produced here, Burrowing Owl Pinot Gris is the perfect wine for pairing with fresh seafood and for summer sipping.

Serves 4

INGREDIENTS

½ cup **Burrowing Owl Pinot Gris**

1 tsp butter

2 tbsp onion, chopped

1 cup 35% cream

1 tbsp basil paste

1 lb goat cheese

8 dried Mission figs, quartered

¼ tsp crushed black pepper

1 tsp garlic, minced

2 tbsp chives, chopped

4 slices prosciutto ham

8 phyllo sheets, halved

6 tbsp olive oil

1. Melt butter in a saucepan, then add onion and sweat until translucent. Add **Burrowing Owl Pinot Gris** and reduce to three-quarters. Add cream and reduce by half. Add the basil paste and blend for 1 minute. Set aside. In a separate bowl mix cheese, figs, pepper, garlic and chives with a wooden spoon until blended. Divide mixture into 4 balls. Wrap each ball in a slice of prosciutto.

2. Preheat oven to 385°F. Brush first 4 of the halved phyllo sheets with olive oil and stack with each corner facing a different direction so that it resembles a 16-point star. Repeat this step 3 more times, making 4 piles of phyllo pastry. Place one ball of cheese mixture in the centre of each phyllo stack. Lift each corner of the phyllo to form a bundle. Squeeze at the top of the ball and pull the corners to form a crown. Place in the oven for 15 minutes.

3. Set baked goat cheese purses in the centre of a plate and lace each purse with 2 tbsp of pesto sauce. Enjoy with a glass of **Burrowing Owl Pinot Gris**.

Burrowing Owl Estate Winery

Location: 100 Burrowing Owl Place (Black Sage Road), Oliver, BC

Telephone (250) 498-0620 **Restaurant Reservations** (250) 498-6202

Website and Email: www.burrowingowlwine.ca, info@burrowingowlwine.ca

Wine Shop, Tours and Tastings: Open daily from Easter until the end of October. Self-guided tours daily and guided tours on weekends.

Getting There: From Highway 97, look for signs between Oliver and Osoyoos at Road 9 or 22.

Highlights: The winery is in a spectacular setting, amidst vineyards that nestle into dramatic black hills and overlook Lake Osoyoos.

The Sonora Room: The restaurant offers fine dining from Easter until Thanksgiving. Fine dining indoors or on the patio is an unforgettable experience.

Whole Artichokes in White Wine

Featuring BC White Wine

The artichoke is probably the world's sexiest vegetable. When selecting an artichoke, look for one that is dark green and heavy. It should have tight leaves. If the leaves are open or it is starting to brown, it is a sign that the artichoke is old and will therefore be tougher.

Serves 2

INGREDIENTS

¼ cup **BC White Wine**

2 tbsp olive oil

4 garlic cloves, crushed

1 bay leaf

1 large lemon, quartered

4 cups chicken or vegetable stock

2 whole artichokes

salt and pepper to taste

1. Combine the **BC White Wine**, olive oil, garlic, bay leaf, 3 lemon quarters, and stock in a large pot. Bring to a simmer over medium heat.

2. To prepare the artichokes, start by running them under cold water. The idea is to remove any grit from between the petals. Cut the stems from the artichokes. Remove the bottom few layers of petals, as they are too tough to eat. Also remove any thorny tips (you may need shears or scissors for this). Cut about 1 inch off the top of the artichoke. Rub the remaining lemon quarter everywhere that the artichoke has been cut.

3. Place the artichokes into the liquid with the bottom facing up. Cover, reduce heat and simmer for 30 minutes. You will know that the artichokes are done when a sharp knife can be inserted through the base of the artichoke without resistance.

4. Serve one artichoke, hot or cold, to each person. To eat, tear off the leaves and scrape off the tender meat with your teeth. Some people like to dip the leaves in a mixture of melted butter and lemon juice; others prefer vinaigrette or even garlic mayonnaise. The heart is the best part, but to get to it you have to remove the inedible hair-like thistles that surround it. This is easy – just lift them up and out.

Opposite: Sonora Room at Burrowing Owl Goat Cheese and Mission Fig Phyllo Purse (Pg 31)
Photo: Gary Faessler

Oysters with a Sparkling Wine Sauce

Featuring BC Dry Sparkling Wine

Fresh raw oysters and sparkling wine are magnificent on their own. However, if you prefer your oysters cooked then this recipe is for you. Pacific Oysters first made an appearance on the table in British Columbia in the 1920's after they were introduced to the coastal waters from Japan. Today between 5000 and 8000 tonnes are harvested in this province every year!

Serves 4

INGREDIENTS

1 cup **BC Dry Sparkling Wine**	1 lb baby spinach
2 tbsp olive oil	1 tbsp butter
2 garlic cloves, crushed	1 tbsp flour
1 lb small oysters, liquor reserved	salt and pepper to taste
½ cup whipping cream	

1. Heat oil in a saucepan over medium heat. Sauté the garlic for about 30 seconds before adding the reserved oyster liquor, **BC Dry Sparkling Wine** and cream. Simmer and reduce the liquid by one-third.

2. Add the oysters and top with baby spinach. Cover and cook for 1-2 minutes until the spinach has wilted. It is important not to overcook the oysters. In a separate small saucepan over medium heat, melt the butter, add flour and combine to form a roux. When well combined, set aside.

3. Remove the spinach and divide it evenly amongst the serving plates. Carefully remove the oysters and place them on the beds of spinach.

4. Add the roux to the sauce to thicken it. Stir well and then pour the sauce over the oysters.

Opposite: Nk'Mip Cellars looking northwest across Osoyoos Lake
Photo: Brian Sprout courtesy of Vincor

Baked Olives in Red Wine

Featuring BC Red Wine

Baking olives in wine is a great way to jazz up your olives. The olives really soak up the flavour of the fennel and wine. Of course, using high quality olives will improve the results.

Serves 4

INGREDIENTS

1 cup **BC Red Wine**

2 cups Kalamata olives, unpitted

½ tsp fennel seeds, crushed

2 garlic cloves, sliced

1 tbsp olive oil

1. Preheat oven to 325°F. In a baking dish, combine olives, **BC Red Wine**, fennel seeds, garlic and olive oil. Bake uncovered for 20 minutes, until olives are heated right through. Every 5 minutes give a stir to ensure that the olives are evenly absorbing the mixture.

2. When the olives are done remove them from the oven and allow to cool for a few minutes before serving. The olives should be served warm, but not hot. This makes a great accompaniment to a cheese plate.

Nk'Mip Steamed Clams

Featuring Nk'Mip Pinot Blanc

This Pinot Blanc recipe was created by Chef Richard Krentz. The wine is bright and lively with an explosion of pineapple and tropical notes followed by a crisp, racy finish. Generous notes of citrus with an underlying mineral nuance complete this well-balanced wine. The Nk'Mip Indian Band, pronounced "Inkameep", were the first people to commercially plant vinifera vineyards in the South Okanagan

Serves 4

INGREDIENTS

1 cup **Nk'Mip Pinot Blanc**	2 garlic cloves, minced
3 dozen clams, well-scrubbed	¼ cup sweet red pepper, chopped
1 tbsp cornmeal	1 tsp lemon zest
3 tbsp unsalted butter	¼ cup cilantro, chopped
2 tbsp olive oil	fresh parsley for garnish

1. Place clams in a large bowl and cover with cold water. Sprinkle with salt and cornmeal and let stand for one hour. Discard water and set clams aside.

2. In a large skillet over medium heat, combine **Nk'Mip Pinot Blanc**, butter, oil, garlic, red peppers and lemon zest. Bring to a simmer, cover and cook for 1 minute.

3. Add clams and cilantro to the skillet. Cook and cover, shaking the skillet 1 or 2 times until the clams open. Discard any clams that do not open.

4. Spoon clams and liquid into 4 shallow bowls and serve. Garnish with fresh parsley. A glass of **Nk'Mip Pinot Blanc** makes a wonderful accompaniment.

Nk'Mip Cellars

Location: 1400 Rancher Creek Road, Osoyoos, BC

Telephone/Fax: (250) 495-2985 / (250) 495-2986

Website: www.nkmipcellars.com

Wine Shop, Tours and Tastings: Open daily summer, spring and fall. Call for tour schedules and special events.

Getting There: Located just off of Highway 3 East on the outskirts of Osoyoos. Well signposted.

Highlights: Nk'Mip Cellars is North America's first aboriginal owned and operated winery. Enjoy many award-winning wines and take in the spectacular views.

VQA

The letters VQA, found on the label of many wines in Canada, stand for Vintners Quality Alliance. There are strict regulations that winemakers must adhere to if they wish to join this alliance.

For example, if the label states "Product of British Columbia" then 100% of the grapes used to make the wine must come from BC. If there is a specific region or viticultural area on the label, then at least 95% of the grapes must come from that region. If a vintage is listed, then 95% of the grapes must come from that harvest year.

It does not end there; once all of these specifications have been met, the wine is subjected to a blind tasting by six professional wine judges. These judges rate the wine and eliminate any wines that do not meet their approval. Only once the wine has satisfied these professional judges is it given the VQA approval. As a result, the VQA approval is recognised as a sign of quality wine.

Wineries in Canada are not obligated to follow VQA standards and there are many wineries that choose not to join for different reasons. Some claim it is too expensive for small wineries to join the Alliance and others just do not want to adhere to a set of rules that they may not agree with.

Baked Crab and Artichoke Dip

Featuring BC White Wine

This appetizer is extremely easy to make and is sure to please any crowd! We usually use Hellmann's mayonnaise, but you can also make your own.

Serves 6

INGREDIENTS

2 tbsp **BC White Wine**

1 can crabmeat (6 oz)

1 jar artichoke hearts (6 oz)

1 cup mayonnaise

1 cup Parmesan cheese, grated

2 garlic cloves, minced

¼ tsp Tabasco sauce

salt and pepper to taste

1. Preheat oven to 350°F. Drain the crab and artichoke hearts well. Combine all ingredients in a food processor and blend well. Transfer to small baking dish and bake for 20-25 minutes, until hot and bubbly.

2. Serve hot with tortilla chips or crusty French bread.

*If you do not have a food processor, chop artichoke hearts and crab and then combine with remaining ingredients in a small bowl before baking.

Mayonnaise

With some practice, this is an easy sauce to make. You can prepare it 2-3 days ahead of time and store it in the fridge in a sealed container. Let it return to room temperature before serving. You can use vegetable oil or olive oil. Vegetable oil makes a lighter sauce, but we prefer to use olive oil with fish. It is very important to have all the ingredients at room temperature when making mayonnaise.

INGREDIENTS

2 egg yolks, at room temperature
salt
1 cup and 2 tbsp vegetable oil or olive oil
2 tbsp lemon juice

1. In a small bowl, beat egg yolks with a pinch of salt until yolks are very pale yellow and the consistency of thick cream. If possible use a blender or an electric beater set at medium speed.

2. Add oil very slowly while beating constantly. Add all of the oil, making a thick mixture.

3. Add lemon juice and salt to taste.

Cheesy Spinach and Wine Dip

Featuring BC White Wine

Many parents and grandparents have terrible memories of spinach. That is because 40 years ago it was generally only available in the canned form. Today we can buy fresh spinach and baby spinach year-round and it tastes nothing like the bitter vegetable that older generations despised. Here it is used in a wonderful cheesy dip, served warm – a great way to stave off the winter blues.

Serves 4-6

INGREDIENTS

3 tbsp butter

¼ cup **BC White Wine**

2 garlic cloves, crushed

1 large bunch of baby spinach

½ cup Hellmann's mayonnaise

3 cups mozzarella cheese, grated

3 green onions, chopped

$^1/_3$ cup half & half

salt and pepper to taste

1. Preheat oven to 350°F. Melt butter in a large sauté pan over medium heat. Add garlic, spinach and **BC White Wine** and stir for 3-4 minutes or until the spinach has completely wilted and wine has reduced by one-third.

2. Remove spinach mixture from heat and transfer to a large bowl. Stir in mayonnaise, cheese, onions, and half & half. Add salt and pepper to taste.

3. Transfer mixture to a small ovenproof dish and bake for 20 minutes.

4. Serve immediately with crusty bread, crackers or tortilla chips.

Cheese Crostini

Featuring BC Red Wine

Someone told us that "crostini" means "little toasts" in Italian. That seems as good a name as any for these fancy little cheese toasts. They go well on a platter at a dinner party and make a fabulous snack.

Makes 10 small toasts

INGREDIENTS

¼ cup **BC Red Wine**

1 egg

2 tbsp whipping cream

1 cup Parmesan cheese, grated

1 small garlic clove

2 tsp fresh parsley

10 baguette slices (½ inch thick)

2 tbsp butter

1. Combine the egg, whipping cream, cheese, garlic and parsley in a food processor or blender and purée until fairly smooth.

2. Spread the purée onto the top of each baguette slice.

3. If your pan is not big enough to hold all of the baguette slices you will have to do 2 batches. In a large frying pan melt the butter over medium heat. As soon as the butter begins to bubble, add the baguette slices with the spread side facing up.

4. When the bottoms of the baguette slices reach a golden brown colour, reduce the heat. Remove the pan from the heat while carefully adding the **BC Red Wine** directly to the pan around the bread. Return the pan to the heat and cover. Cook for about 5 minutes until cheese has melted.

5. Serve immediately.

Pentâge Coquilles St Jacques

Featuring Pentâge Pinot Gris

Pentâge is a boutique farm-gate winery on 23 acres overlooking Skaha Lake in Penticton. Our low-yield vineyard strategy produces the top quality grapes essential to the creation of our handcrafted, limited release, premium wines. Our Pinot Gris is a dry, fruit-forward wine with alluring stone fruit aromas. It is the perfect accompaniment for seafood. These flavours are splendidly showcased in this fresh take on a classic recipe.

Serves 6-8

INGREDIENTS

1½ cups **Pentâge Pinot Gris**	1 cup Gruyère cheese, grated
2 shallots, finely chopped	½ lb cooked shrimp
1 bay leaf	½ cup whipping cream
1 lb large scallops	¼ cup fine dry breadcrumbs
3 tbsp butter	½ cup Parmesan cheese, grated
8 mushrooms, sliced	salt and fresh ground pepper to taste
3 tbsp flour	

1. Pour **Pentâge Pinot Gris** into a saucepan and add shallots and bay leaf. Bring to a boil and add scallops. Return to boil, then cover and reduce heat immediately, simmering for 5 minutes. Remove scallops and set aside. Discard bay leaf and reserve liquid for later use.

2. Melt butter in a separate pan over medium heat and sauté mushrooms until golden brown. Add flour and stir until combined thoroughly. Add reserved poaching liquid slowly, stirring continuously. When all poaching liquid has been added, stir in Gruyère cheese, shrimp and cream. Mixture should be thick and bubbly. Add salt and fresh ground pepper to taste.

3. Place scallops in individual coquille dishes, au gratin dishes or ramekins. Spoon sauce over the scallops. Sprinkle breadcrumbs and Parmesan cheese over the sauce. Place shells or dishes under the broiler for 3 minutes or until crumbs are golden brown.

4. Serve immediately. This dish is wonderful served with a glass of **Pentâge Pinot Gris**.

Pentâge Winery

Location: 4400 Lakeside Road, Penticton, BC

Telephone: (250) 493-4008

Website and Email: www.pentage.com, pentage@vip.net

Wine Shop, Tours and Tastings: Wine shop and tasting room by appointment.

Getting There: Head south on South Main Road out of Penticton. This turns into Lakeside Road. The entrance to 4400 Lakeside Road is on your left. Well signposted.

Highlights: The view!! This is one of the most spectacular vineyard locations in North America, if not the world! Bring your camera.

Thai Fishcakes with Sweet Chilli Dipping Sauce

Featuring BC Icewine

Thai food has developed into one of the world's most distinctive and sought-after cuisines. It comes from a combination of influences, including chillies brought by Portuguese traders, Indian spices and curries, and the Chinese method of cooking with a wok. If you have never tried Thai fishcakes, prepare to have your socks knocked off because these are fantastic. We made this delicious sauce without the fresh chillies using a chilli-infused icewine from Silver Sage called "The Flame", but the recipe provided below will work with any icewine.

Serves 4

INGREDIENTS

¼ cup **BC Icewine**

1 tbsp fresh chillies, chopped (to taste)

2 tbsp rice wine vinegar

4 tbsp fish sauce

1½ tbsp lime juice

1 garlic clove, crushed

1 lb boneless, skinless white fish fillets

¼ tsp salt

½ cup cilantro

1 egg

2 tsp red curry paste (to taste)

2 green onions, chopped

½ cup canola oil

1. To make the dipping sauce, combine **BC Icewine**, chillies, rice wine vinegar, 2 tbsp fish sauce, ½ tbsp lime juice and crushed garlic in a small bowl. Stir well and set aside.

2. Place fish and salt in a food processor for 15 seconds or until it forms a paste. Add cilantro, egg, red curry paste and remaining fish sauce and lime juice. Process for 15 additional seconds or until well combined. Transfer to a bowl, add green onions and mix well.

3. Heat oil in a wok or frying pan over medium-high heat. With wet hands to prevent sticking, take 2 heaped tbsp of mixture and roll into a ball. Flatten into a patty and place in pan; repeat until all of the mixture is gone. Make at least 8 patties. Cook 3 or 4 patties at a time until golden brown on each side.

4. Serve these delicious Thai fishcakes with the sweet chilli dipping sauce. This sauce is also great with spring rolls, crab cakes or Vietnamese noodle dishes!

Salads

If food is the body of good living, wine is its soul.

Clifton Fadiman 1902-1999

Crumbed Goat Cheese and Walnut Salad

Caesar Salad

Mixed Green Salad with Icewine Poppy Seed Dressing

Strawberry and Spinach Salad

Organic Greens with Toasted Pine Nuts, Feta and Blueberry Vinaigrette

Crumbed Goat Cheese and Walnut Salad

Featuring BC Pinot Gris

This salad has a wonderful mixture of textures and flavours that will have your guests begging for more. Walnuts and goat cheese compliment each other in any recipe and this one is no exception. We used Blue Grouse Pinot Gris to create this recipe and the results were superb.

Serves 4-8

INGREDIENTS

½ cup **BC Pinot Gris**

½ cup walnuts, chopped

2 pinches of salt

2 garlic cloves, crushed

1 tbsp Dijon mustard

2 tbsp fresh dill, chopped

3 tbsp olive oil

1 log of goat cheese (10-12 oz)

1 egg

½ cup fine breadcrumbs

12 cups mixed salad greens

1. Preheat oven to 350°F. Place walnuts on a baking sheet and bake for 5-10 minutes or until brown and toasty. Be careful not to burn. Set aside to cool.

2. While walnuts are browning put 1 pinch of salt and garlic in a bowl. Using the back of a spoon, mash the garlic and the salt together until it forms a paste. Add mustard, dill, 2 tbsp oil and **BC Pinot Gris**. Whisk together well.

3. Cut goat cheese log into ¼ inch discs. Beat the egg in a small bowl. Put breadcrumbs mixed with another pinch of salt on a plate. Coat each disc in egg, then breadcrumbs.

4. Add remaining oil to a sauté pan over medium heat. Sauté the cheese disks in oil for 2-3 minutes on each side or until they are golden brown on the outside and creamy in the middle. Remove disks and place on absorbent paper.

5. Distribute salad greens evenly among the plates. Drizzle with dressing and top with cheese discs and walnuts. Serve immediately and accompany with a glass of **BC Pinot Gris**.

Pinot Gris

Pronounced (pee-no-gree)

Pinot Gris is a mutation of the Pinot Noir grape. It is known as Pinot Grigio in Italy, Tokay d'Alsace in France and Grauburgunder or Rülander in Germany. Originally from Burgundy, it has been around since the Middle Ages. "Gris" means grey in French and this refers to the colour often found in the grapes. In British Columbia the colour of the grapes ranges from bluish grey to pinkish brown.

The Heiss family first planted the grape in British Columbia in the early 1980s. Since then it has become very popular with British Columbian wine drinkers. The northern climate is perfect for the grape and the natural acidity in the soil produces clean fresh flavours in the wine. In hotter climates the grape does not seem to do as well.

Pinot Gris can be either tangy and light or rich and full-bodied depending on the ripeness of the grapes and on the techniques used to create the wine. The wine is full of lively flavours and generally contains aromas of fresh fruits such as pear, melon and apple.

This wine is wonderful paired with fish and seafood and is great with sushi. It will also hold up against strong cheeses such as brie and even stilton.

Caesar Salad

Featuring BC White Wine

This crisp salad served with a creamy garlic dressing can be served as a meal or as a side dish. You may find that you have extra dressing, which you can store for up to 2 days. You can also use the dressing as a marinade for grilled meats.

Serves 6

INGREDIENTS

¼ cup **BC White Wine**

4 garlic cloves, crushed

1 egg yolk at room temperature

1 tbsp lemon juice

½ tbsp Worcestershire sauce

2 tsp anchovy paste

¾ cup olive oil

1 large head Romaine lettuce

2 cups croutons

½ cup Parmesan cheese, grated

salt and ground pepper to taste

1. Mix garlic, egg yolk, lemon juice, Worcestershire sauce, anchovy paste, salt and pepper in a blender (or use an electric mixer). Blend until smooth. Add oil in a slow stream while continuously mixing. Remove mixture from the blender and stir in **BC White Wine** to thin to your taste. Chill about 2 hours.

2. Tear lettuce into bite-size pieces and add to a large salad bowl. Toss lettuce with dressing and croutons. Sprinkle with Parmesan cheese and serve immediately.

Croutons

This basic crouton recipe is delicious served with Caesar salad or other green salads.

Makes about 2 cups

INGREDIENTS

2 tbsp butter or garlic butter
3 cups day-old bread, crusts removed and cubed (½ inch cubes)
3 tbsp Parmesan cheese, finely grated

1. Preheat oven to 350°F.

2. Melt butter in a large skillet over moderate heat until it foams. Add bread cubes and toss to coat with melted butter. Immediately add Parmesan cheese and toss well to melt cheese slightly.

3. Transfer cubes to baking sheets and bake until croutons are crisp and golden but still soft inside, about 15-20 minutes. Check and turn occasionally.

Mixed Green Salad with Icewine Poppy Seed Dressing

Featuring BC Icewine

Poppy seeds have been used in cooking for hundreds of years. They are often found in cakes and breads throughout Europe, in desserts in Turkey and in salad dressings in North America. The tiny poppy seeds give the dressing a wonderful texture and they look great too. It is estimated that it takes about 900,000 poppy seeds to make up a pound.

Serves 4-6

INGREDIENTS

½ cup **BC Icewine** or **Late Harvest Wine**

¼ cup red wine vinegar

½ tsp dry mustard

½ tsp paprika

2 tbsp poppy seeds

½ cup vegetable oil

1 lb mixed salad greens

1 cup red seedless grapes, halved lengthwise

½ red onion, diced

1 yellow pepper, sliced into strips

1 ripe avocado, sliced

salt and pepper to taste

1. Combine the **BC Icewine**, vinegar, mustard, paprika, poppy seeds, oil, salt and pepper in a bowl and whisk.

2. Toss the salad greens, grapes, onion and yellow pepper with the dressing and distribute evenly amongst the serving plates. Top with avocado slices and serve.

Chef's Tip

For a simple way to make a dressing that requires whisking, just add all of the ingredients to a jar or sealed container and shake it vigorously. This generally works better than using a whisk and it is much more convenient than using a blender or food processor.

Strawberry and Spinach Salad

Featuring BC White Wine

"Summer in a bowl" is how one friend has described this attractive and delicious salad. This dressing also stores well in the fridge if you want to make extra. Occasionally we add feta cheese as it provides an exciting combination of sweet and salty.

Serves 6-8

INGREDIENTS

1 cup **BC White Wine**

$^1/_3$ cup shallots, minced

$^1/_3$ cup liquid honey

1 tbsp raspberry vinegar

2 tsp Dijon mustard

¼ cup vegetable oil

12 oz fresh baby spinach

2 cups fresh strawberries, sliced

8 button mushrooms, sliced

salt to taste

1. In a small saucepan over medium heat, combine **BC White Wine** and shallots. Bring to a boil, then simmer for 12-15 minutes or until reduced to a syrup-like consistency.

2. Transfer wine mixture to a small bowl and whisk with honey, vinegar, mustard and salt. Slowly add the oil while you whisk until mixture is well-combined and thickened.

3. In a large salad bowl combine the spinach, strawberries and mushrooms and toss with the dressing.

Opposite: Red Rooster's Goat Cheese and Red Pepper Penne (Pg 134)
Photo: Gary Faessler

Organic Greens with Toasted Pine Nuts, Feta and Blueberry Vinaigrette

Featuring BC Blueberry Wine

The unusual colour of the dressing makes this salad very appealing to the eye. With wonderful textures and a fabulous combination of salty and sweet, this salad will satisfy your every desire.

Serves 4-6

INGREDIENTS

¾ cup **BC Blueberry Wine**

1 garlic clove, crushed

1 tbsp sugar

¼ cup apple cider vinegar

1 tbsp Dijon mustard

½ cup canola oil

½ cup pine nuts

12 cups mixed organic greens

½ cup feta cheese, crumbled

1. Mix the **BC Blueberry Wine**, sugar and garlic in a small saucepan over medium heat. Bring to a boil then reduce heat and simmer for 15 minutes.

2. Transfer mixture to a food processor or blender and add the vinegar and mustard. While blending, slowly add the canola oil.

3. In a dry pan over medium heat toast the pine nuts. Stir frequently, making sure not to burn them.

4. Divide the greens evenly between the plates. Top with pine nuts and crumbled feta cheese and drizzle with blueberry vinaigrette.

Opposite: Gourmet Sloppy Joes "Nichol Style" (Pg 124)
Photo: Gary Faessler

Soups & Stews

Drink a glass of wine after your soup and you steal a ruble from your doctor.

Old Russian proverb

Church & State's Oyster Cream Soup Garnished with Oyster Beignet

Honeydew and Icewine Soup

Shrimp Bisque

Recline Ridge's Fish Stew

Creamy Pumpkin and Apple Soup

Traditional Clam Chowder

Glenterra's Lavender-Blueberry Soup

Cream of Mushroom Soup

Pôchouse

Venison Stew

Sparkling Okanagan Peach Soup

Larch Hills Hearty Beef Bourguignon

Church & State's Oyster Cream Soup Garnished with Oyster Beignet

Featuring Classic White

Caterers Feys & Hobbs have come up with this delicious treat utilising Church & State's Classic White. Pinot Blanc forms the backbone of this blend. Chardonnay was added for roundness and mouth feel, and a bit of Riesling for acidity. It was blended as a food wine that can accompany a wide range of dishes, from shellfish and seafood to chicken and light pastas.

Serves 8

INGREDIENTS

1 cup **Classic White**

4 tbsp butter

3 shallots, sliced

2 garlic cloves, crushed

16 oysters, shucked, liquor reserved

4 cups chicken or vegetable stock

4 cups whipping cream

4 cups nasturtium leaf of arugula

(or substitute watercress)

nasturtium blossoms for garnish

1. Melt butter in a saucepan over medium heat. Sweat shallots for 2 minutes until they smell sweet and start to brown. Add garlic and cook an additional 30 seconds. Add oysters, keeping the liquor reserved. Cook until the edges curl; a bit of colour on the oysters is okay.

2. Deglaze the pan with the **Classic White** and oyster liquor, allowing it to reduce by half. Add the stock and cream and bring to a hard boil. Simmer and allow to reduce by about one-third.

3. Pour into a blender (one or two batches), add the nasturtium leaf and blend on high for 1 minute until smooth. Pour back into the pot to re-heat. Adjust seasoning if desired. Serve in warmed bowls and garnish with nasturtium leaves, blossoms and oyster beignet (next page).

Church & State Wines

Location: 1445 Benvenuto Avenue, Brentwood Bay, BC

Telephone: (250) 652-2671

Website: www.churchandstatewines.com

Wine Shop, Tours and Tastings: The winery welcomes visitors for tours and tastings. Please call ahead for current times.

Getting There: Follow Highway 17 (Pat Bay Highway) and turn left at Keating X Road. Continue past the West Saanich Road intersection. The winery is on the left.

Highlights: Learn about the process of winemaking, watch food prepared with local farm fresh ingredients in an open-style kitchen or simply enjoy lunch on the deck overlooking the vineyard. As you depart, be sure to stop by the marketplace for many of the items sampled on your visit.

Oyster Beignet

The beignets can also be served as an appetiser in their own right.

INGREDIENTS

8 oysters, shucked and blotted dry
½ cup flour, plus some for dusting
¼ cup cornstarch
2 tsp baking powder
2 egg whites

1 dash BC sparkling wine, milk or
iced water
3 tbsp oil
sea salt to taste

1. In a small bowl mix together the flour, cornstarch and baking powder. In a separate bowl whisk the egg whites until frothy. Add the egg white to the dry ingredients and fold together. Add a splash of BC sparkling wine, milk or ice water to adjust the consistency to that of a thick pancake batter.

2. In another small bowl toss the blotted oysters with a tbsp of flour. Dip the dusted oysters in the prepared batter and slip them into a shallow frying pan with hot oil preheated to 350°F.

3. Fry oysters until golden brown on both sides, remove and blot on paper towel. Serve 2 oysters per guest as a garnish for the soup or as hors d'oeuvres with a dip.

Honeydew and Icewine Soup

Featuring BC Icewine

This delicious summer treat is unbeatable on a hot day. It makes a great start to a meal or a wonderful snack on its own. If you are going on a picnic it will keep cool in a thermos.

Serves 4

INGREDIENTS

½ cup **BC Icewine**

2 honeydew melons

¼ cup freshly squeezed lime juice

½ cup fresh mint leaves, chopped

1. Cut honeydew melons in half and remove the seeds. Carefully scoop out the flesh without damaging the outside of the melon. The rind will be used as a serving bowl.

2. Place melon, lime juice and mint into a blender or food processor and pulse into a purée.

3. Pour the mixture through a strainer to remove the pulp. Add **BC Icewine** and stir well. Cover and refrigerate for 1-2 hours.

4. Pour the soup into the hollow melon husks and serve with a glass of **BC Icewine**.

Icewine

In the late 1700s winemakers in Franconia, Germany, were alarmed to find that an extreme cold spell had left their grapes frozen on the vines. They decided not to lose the harvest and went ahead pressing the juice from the frozen grapes. The results left them dumbfounded; they had just made the world's first icewine.

Canada's first icewine was produced in British Columbia by Walter Hainle in 1978. Walter remembered tasting icewine while he was growing up in Germany and he wanted to recreate a similar wine in Canada.

The grapes used to make icewine must be handpicked in extremely cold temperatures, between -8 and -13 degrees Celsius. To ensure the grapes are completely frozen, the temperature must have been at this level for at least 24 hours. When pressed in this state, because the water in the grape is still ice, only a few precious drops of extremely sweet, concentrated liquid can be extracted. This juice is allowed to settle before it is clarified and fermented.

It usually takes a lot more grapes to produce a single 200ml bottle of icewine than it does to produce a regular 750ml bottle of wine. This is one of the reasons that icewine is more expensive than other types of wine; it is just so expensive to make.

Icewine is always sweet, yet each grape variety retains its own characteristics. Icewine should be served chilled but not cold. 10-12 degrees Celsius is often believed to be the ideal temperature. Most icewines should be consumed while they are young, though a notable exception is Riesling, which has proven to cellar well. Once opened, a bottle will last 3-5 days in the refrigerator, as long as it has been re-corked.

Shrimp Bisque

Featuring BC White Wine

This soup tastes nothing like the canned varieties you may have tried. This is real shrimp bisque with real shrimp flavour. Even the shells are used to provide extra flavour. When straining, it is easiest to put the cheesecloth inside a metal strainer and pour in the liquid, pressing through as much juice as possible.

Serves 4

INGREDIENTS

¾ cup **BC White Wine**

2 tbsp butter

1 small carrot, chopped

½ onion, chopped

1 bay leaf

½ tsp dried thyme

15 large raw shrimp, unpeeled

½ cup flour

4 cups chicken or fish stock

2 tbsp cream

1. Melt butter in a heavy pan over medium heat. Sauté carrot and onion with bay leaf and thyme until vegetables are soft. Add **BC White Wine** and shrimp and poach for 8-10 minutes. Remove the shrimp from the pan and set aside.

2. Peel 8 shrimp, reserving the shells. Dice the meat and set aside for garnish. Put the shells and the remaining unshelled shrimp in a food processor and blend into a paste.

3. Slowly stir the shrimp paste into the poaching liquid then add the flour and mix well. Add the stock and return to a boil and then simmer for 15 minutes. Strain the soup through a sieve and then cheesecloth before adding cream and reheating.

4. Serve into individual bowls and then add the diced shrimp meat to garnish.

Siegerrebe

THIS WINE WAS DEVELOPED AT THE ALZEY INSTITUTE IN GERMANY AT THE BEGINNING OF THE LAST CENTURY. IT IS A CROSS BETWEEN GEWÜRZTRAMINER AND THE MADELEINE ANGEVINE VARIETIES OF GRAPE. IT IS STILL GROWN IN GERMANY BUT ONLY IN LIMITED AMOUNTS.

THIS VARIETY IS VERY SUSCEPTIBLE TO WASPS AND BIRDS, THAT ARE ATTRACTED TO THE EARLY RIPENING FRUIT. MANY CROPS HAVE SUFFERED FROM THE ATTACKS OF THESE WINGED PREDATORS, BUT WINEMAKERS CONTINUE TO BATTLE AGAINST THE ELEMENTS TO PRODUCE THE WONDERFUL WINE THAT COMES FROM THE GRAPE.

IN BRITISH COLUMBIA QUITE A FEW WINEMAKERS AND WINE LOVERS HAVE LISTED THIS RELATIVELY UNKNOWN VARIETY OF WINE AS THEIR ALL-TIME FAVOURITE.

SIEGERREBE PAIRS VERY WELL WITH CHEESE, FRUIT, SEAFOOD, POULTRY AND DISHES THAT ARE MODERATELY SPICED. SO DON'T WORRY IF YOU STILL CAN'T PRONOUNCE IT; THAT'S NOT IMPORTANT, ALL YOU HAVE TO DO IS ENJOY IT.

Recline Ridge's Fish Stew

Featuring Recline Ridge Siegerrebe

The Recline Ridge Siegerrebe has been very successful, with numerous vintages receiving medals at the Pacific Northwest Wine Summit and the All Canadian Championships. The winery overlooks the vineyard and is framed by Tappen Mountain and the Tappen and Skimikin Valleys.

Serves 6

INGREDIENTS

1 big splash of **Recline Ridge Siegerrebe**

3 leeks, julienned (white part only)

¼ cup onion, finely chopped

5 garlic cloves, minced

2 bay leaves, pulverised

¼ tsp freshly ground black pepper

¼ cup green pepper, diced small

1 pinch dried fennel, ground

1 can tomatoes, drained (14 oz)

1 tsp orange zest

1 pinch celery seed

2½ cups water

$^1/_3$ cup whipping cream

5 small potatoes, peeled and cut into sixths

3 lbs fish fillets (cubed to 1 inch)

2 oz smoked fish (more to taste)

2 tsp salt

2 tbsp tomato paste

½ cup frozen peas

½ tsp Chiles Chipoltes (smoked chilli peppers)

1. In a saucepan combine the leeks, onion, garlic, bay leaves, pepper, green pepper, fennel, tomatoes, orange zest and celery seed. Bring to a simmer until the onions are translucent.

2. Transfer the ingredients from the saucepan to a stockpot and add water, cream, potatoes, fish pieces, smoked fish, salt, tomato paste, peas, and smoked chillies. Top off with a generous splash of **Recline Ridge Siegerrebe**. Bring to a simmer for about 30 minutes or until fish is cooked and potatoes are tender. Enjoy with a glass of **Recline Ridge Siegerrebe**.

Recline Ridge Vineyards and Winery

Location: 2640 Skimikin Road, Tappen, BC

Telephone/Fax: (250) 835-2212 / (250) 835-2228

Website and Email: www.recline-ridge.bc.ca, inquiry@recline-ridge.bc.ca

Wine Shop, Tours and Tastings: Tasting room and wine shop open daily Apr, May, Jun, Oct noon-5pm and Jul-Sep 10am-5pm

Getting There: Take the Trans-Canada Highway west of Salmon Arm. At 14.4km from the Centenoka Mall, turn south on Tappen Valley Road. Proceed 4km to Skimikin Road.

Highlights: Visitors to the wine shop will enjoy a warm reception in the serenity of the beautiful post and beam winery building.

Creamy Pumpkin and Apple Soup

Featuring BC Dry White Wine

This unusual combination of ingredients is sure to surprise any soup lover. The flavours are wonderful. It is a soup that you will make again and again.

Serves 4

INGREDIENTS

½ cup **BC Dry White Wine**

3 tbsp butter

1 lb pumpkin, peeled, seeded and chopped

1 lb Granny Smith apples, peeled, cored and chopped

1 tsp curry powder

1 onion, diced

4 cups chicken or vegetable stock

1 cup whipping cream

salt and black pepper to taste

chopped chives to garnish

1. Melt butter in large pot over medium heat. Add pumpkin, apples, onion and curry. Stir 4-5 minutes until onion is soft. Add stock and **BC Dry White Wine**.

2. Turn up heat and bring soup to the boiling point, then reduce heat and simmer for 30 minutes or until pumpkin is very soft.

3. Remove soup from the heat and let it cool before transferring it to a food processor or blender. Purée the soup and return to the pot.

4. Gently reheat soup, being careful not to boil. When soup is hot, add cream and stir for another minute. Add salt and pepper to taste. Transfer soup to individual serving bowls and garnish with fresh chives.

Traditional Clam Chowder

Featuring BC White Wine

Sailors and fisherman have enjoyed clam chowder for hundreds of years. The French and English fisherman who plied their trade off of the Newfoundland coast probably brought it to Canada sometime during the 1500s. This traditional recipe is similar to that mentioned in Herman Melville's classic adventure Moby Dick written in 1851.

Serves 4

INGREDIENTS

1½ cups **BC White Wine**

4 slices bacon

2 tbsp olive oil

4 sprigs fresh thyme

1 bay leaf

2 onions, chopped

4 garlic cloves, crushed

36 littleneck clams, scrubbed clean

1 tbsp fresh lemon juice

2 cups water

¼ cup flour

1 tbsp butter

2 cups whipping cream

2 large potatoes, peeled and diced

salt and pepper to taste

¼ cup flat leaf parsley, chopped for garnish

1. Cook the bacon for about 5 minutes in a large saucepan over medium heat until the fat has rendered and the bacon is browned. Remove the cooked bacon, let it cool, then chop it into pieces and set it aside. Add 1 tbsp of olive oil and the thyme, bay leaf, half of the crushed garlic and half of the chopped onion. Sauté for another 5 minutes, until the onion is translucent.

2. Add half of the clams, **BC White Wine**, lemon juice and water and bring to a boil. Reduce heat to a simmer, cover the pot and leave for 10-12 minutes, until the clams are opened. Remove the clams from the pot and discard any that did not open. Strain the broth into a bowl and set aside.

3. Take the cooked clams and remove the meat from the shell. Chop the meat into pieces and set it aside. Discard the empty shells.

4. Heat the butter and remaining olive oil in a large pot over medium heat. Add the remaining onion and garlic and sauté for 8 minutes or until the onion is soft. Add the flour and stir it through well. Add the chopped bacon and pour in the strained broth.

5. Add cream and diced potatoes and bring to a boil for 7-8 minutes, stirring while the mixture is boiling. The potatoes should be very soft – it is great if they begin to break down as this will only add to the creamy thick texture of the chowder. Add the chopped clam meat and season with salt and pepper to taste.

6. Finally, add the remaining clams in their shells. Cover the pot and simmer for 10 minutes, until the shells open. Again, discard any clams that did not open. Garnish with parsley before serving.

Glenterra's Lavender-Blueberry Soup

Featuring Glenterra Brio

The Brio used in this recipe is a hearty red blend that contains 10 different grape varieties. It has been aged in both American and French oak. This recipe won a local cooking with lavender competition and features fresh fruits, herbs and vegetables produced in the Cowichan Valley. It can be served hot or cold; we prefer it cold with a glass of Glenterra's Vivace wine. This fruity, slightly sweet, crisp white blend amplifies the fruity-floral notes in the soup.

Serves 4

INGREDIENTS

1 cup **Glenterra Brio**	1 large lemon, juiced and zested
2 quarts blueberries	1 cinnamon stick (4 inches)
1½ cups water	½ tsp ground black pepper
¾ cup honey (adjust to taste)	½ tsp ground cloves
¼ cup fresh orange juice	1 dollop crème fraîche
1½ tbsp dried lavender flowers	mint sprigs to garnish

1. In a large saucepan combine the **Glenterra Brio** with all of the ingredients, except ¼ cup blueberries, crème fraîche and mint.

2. Bring to a boil and then reduce heat and simmer for 8 minutes. Remove the cinnamon stick. Garnish with a dollop of crème fraîche, a sprinkling of fresh blueberries and a mint sprig.

Glenterra Vineyards

Location: 3897 Cobble Hill Road, Cobble Hill, BC

Telephone: (250) 743-2330

Email: glenterravineyards@shaw.ca

Wine Shop, Tours and Tastings: Winery is open Mar-Oct, daily 11am-6pm; winter noon-5pm, or by chance. Sample handcrafted wines.

Getting There: Winery is located about 10km south of Duncan, off of the Trans-Canada Highway. Head east on Cobble Hill Road at the stoplight by the Valley View Centre. The winery is only 1 minute down the road.

Highlights: With spectacular scenery, you are invited to take a self-guided tour and view the 10-year-old vineyard growing around 40 varieties.

Cream of Mushroom Soup

Featuring BC White Wine

This recipe highlights the beautiful marriage that occurs between mushrooms and wine. Use whatever mushrooms are in season in your area. British Columbia is abundant with wild mushrooms and it is great fun to head out for a days pickings. Be sure to pack a field guide so you can identify the edible species or go with an experienced mushroom picker. Even people who say they do not like mushroom, have loved this recipe.

Serves 2-4

INGREDIENTS

1 cup **BC White Wine**

3 tbsp olive oil

4 garlic cloves, crushed

2 cups mushrooms, finely chopped

½ cup vegetable stock

3 tbsp butter

3 tbsp flour

2 cups milk

salt and pepper to taste

1. Heat oil in a medium-sized saucepan over medium heat. Add garlic and sauté for 1 minute before adding mushrooms. Cook until the mushrooms are soft. Add **BC White Wine** and stock and bring to a boil. As soon as it boils reduce heat and simmer for 15 minutes.

2. While soup is simmering, in a separate small saucepan melt butter over medium heat. Add flour and mix well. Slowly add the milk, stirring quickly. Let it cook 3-5 minutes, stirring continuously, until the mixture thickens into a white sauce.

3. Add the white sauce to the wine and mushroom mixture. Combine thoroughly; if it is too thick add extra milk. Add salt and pepper to taste. Serve with crusty French bread.

Pôchouse

Featuring BC Chardonnay

You may be asking, what on earth is a Pôchouse? It is a traditional freshwater fish stew from the Burgundy region of France. Pronounced poh-hahz, it comes from the word "fisherman" in the old Burgundy dialect. After trying this delectable treat in France it was an absolute necessity to include a version of it here.

Serves 4

INGREDIENTS

2½ cups **BC Chardonnay**	½ cup mushrooms, sliced
½ tsp dried thyme	2 onions, chopped
½ tsp fennel seeds	3 garlic cloves, chopped
2 bay leaves	¼ cup flour
6 tbsp butter	4 lbs fresh water fish fillets, cut into
6 oz bacon, diced	chunks (trout, walleye, pike, etc.)

1. Wrap up the thyme, fennel and bay leaves in a piece of cheesecloth to form a bouquet garni. Tie it up very securely.

2. In a large pot melt 2 tbsp butter over medium heat. Add bacon and sauté until browned. Add onions, garlic and mushrooms, stirring well for 5 minutes. Add the fish and the **BC Chardonnay**. If fish is not completely covered then top up with more wine.

3. Add the bouquet garni and bring to a simmer for 10-12 minutes or until fish is cooked. Once cooked, remove the fish from the broth and set aside in a warm dish.

4. In a separate bowl combine the flour with the remaining butter and work it into a paste. Add one-quarter of the broth and mix well. When it is thoroughly combined, return this to the big pot of broth and stir. Cook for another 10 minutes.

5. Discard the bouquet garni and pour the broth over the fish. Serve the dish with a glass of **BC Chardonnay**. Just like being in Burgundy, France!

Bouquet Garni

A bouquet garni is a collection of herbs that are bundled together to flavour your dish. They are either wrapped in cheesecloth or tied together. The traditional bouquet garni consists of parsley, thyme and bay leaves but like the recipe above, you can modify this to suit your taste.

A basic bouquet garni consists of:

2 tsp dried parsley
1 tsp dried thyme
2 bay leaves

Cooking with BC Wine

Venison Stew

Featuring BC Red Wine

Compared to beef and lamb, venison is low in calories, fat and cholesterol. Here it is used to make an easy-to-prepare stew that will help fight off those winter blues. If you do not have access to wild deer then any good butcher should stock venison. Back in 1990 most of the venison sold in British Columbia was imported from New Zealand. Today, around 80 BC fallow deer farms serve more than 80% of the local market.

Serves 6

INGREDIENTS

1 cup **BC Red Wine**	2 cups onion, chopped
¼ cup flour	1 cup celery, chopped
½ tbsp paprika	1 cup carrots, chopped
½ tbsp salt	3 garlic cloves, chopped
½ tbsp garlic powder	1½ cups fresh tomatoes, chopped
1 tsp black pepper	1 tbsp fresh basil, chopped
½ tbsp onion powder	1 tbsp fresh thyme, chopped
½ tbsp cayenne pepper	1 bay leaf
½ tbsp dried oregano	4 cups beef stock
2 lbs venison, chopped into chunks	salt and pepper to taste
3 tbsp olive oil	

1. In a mixing bowl combine flour, paprika, salt, garlic powder, black pepper, onion powder, cayenne pepper and dried oregano. Coat the meat in this mixture.

2. In a large pot, heat oil over high heat. When the oil is hot, add the meat, stirring and searing for 3 minutes. Reduce heat to medium and add the onions, sautéing for 2 minutes. Then add the celery and carrots and cook for another 2 minutes. Add the garlic, tomatoes, basil, thyme and the bay leaf and stir for 1 minute.

3. Deglaze the pan with the **BC Red Wine** then add the stock. Bring to a boil then reduce heat to simmer. Cover and let the stew simmer for 50 minutes to 1 hour or until meat is very tender. If the liquid reduces too much add a little more stock or wine. Make sure that if you add wine, let it simmer for a while longer before serving.

Opposite: Mt Boucherie's Mouth Watering Sundried Tomato Salmon Fillets (Pg 92)
Photo: Gary Faessler

Sparkling Okanagan Peach Soup

Featuring BC Sparkling Wine

Fresh Okanagan peaches are one of the world's finest fruits. Here they are combined with BC Sparkling Wine to make an unforgettable summer soup. This is a dish that will surprise and delight your dinner guests and have them begging you for the recipe.

Serves 6

INGREDIENTS

1¼ cups **BC Sparkling Wine**, chilled

3 lbs fresh peaches, peeled and chopped

½ cup peach nectar

1 tbsp sugar

¼ cup water

¼ tsp cinnamon

1½ tbsp lemon juice

¼ cup fresh mint leaves

fresh mint sprigs for garnish

1. Combine peaches, nectar, water, sugar, lemon juice and cinnamon in a saucepan over high heat. Bring to a boil and then reduce to simmer. Cover and simmer for 15 minutes or until peaches are soft. Remove from heat and set aside to cool.

2. Pour mixture into a blender, add mint and process until smooth. Pour mixture into a bowl, cover and refrigerate for 2 hours or until the mixture is chilled throughout.

3. Just before serving, add the **BC Sparkling Wine** and stir gently. Serve the soup in individual bowls, each decorated with a sprig of mint.

Opposite: Court Faessler in the vineyard at River's Bend Winery
Photo: Linda Faessler

Cooking with BC Wine

Larch Hills Hearty Beef Bourguignon

Featuring Larch Hills Pinot Noir

This Pinot Noir is spicy with ruby colour and medium body. It has berry flavours, smooth tannins and very light oak with a slight black pepper finish. Super with meat dishes or try it slightly chilled with prawns and pasta.

Serves 6-8

INGREDIENTS

2 cups **Larch Hills Pinot Noir**

¾ lb mushrooms, sliced

3 tbsp butter

2 medium onions, chopped

3 tbsp shortening

3 lbs boneless beef chuck, cut into 2 inch cubes

3 tbsp flour

1 can beef broth or stock (10 oz)

1 tbsp tomato paste

4 garlic cloves, minced

1 tsp dried thyme

1 bay leaf

salt and fresh ground pepper to taste

4 parsley sprigs plus some for garnish

1. Preheat oven to 350°F. In a large skillet, sauté mushrooms lightly in butter. Remove and set aside. Add shortening to pan and brown onions well over moderate heat. Remove and set aside with mushrooms. Add beef chunks in small batches, browning them well on all sides. Add extra fat if needed. Remove beef to a heavy 4 or 5 quart ovenproof casserole dish.

2. To the fat remaining in the skillet, stir in flour, and then beef stock, **Larch Hills Pinot Noir** and tomato paste. Bring to a boil, stirring constantly as sauce thickens. Add garlic, thyme, salt, pepper, parsley and bay leaf. Now is a great time for a sip of Pinot Noir! Pour sauce over beef in casserole. It should almost cover the beef – add more wine if necessary. Cover casserole tightly and bake in the oven for 2-3 hours or until meat is tender. Gently stir in mushrooms and onions. Bake 20-30 minutes longer.

3. Taste sauce, adjusting if necessary. Garnish with chopped parsley. Serve directly from casserole, with French bread and a glass of **Larch Hills Pinot Noir**.

Larch Hills Estate Winery

Location: 110 Timms Road, Salmon Arm, BC

Telephone/Fax: (250) 832-0155 / (250) 832-9419

Website and Email: www.larchhillswinery.com, info@larchhillswinery.com

Wine Shop, Tours and Tastings: Winery is open for viewing, tasting and sales Apr 1-Oct 31, daily noon-5pm. Group tours by appointment.

Getting There: from the north, drive south on Highway 97B. 1 km past the golf course, turn left onto Black Road. Follow signage and turn right on Timms Road. Winery is 4km from the highway about 15km southeast of Salmon Arm.

Highlights: Specialising in cool climate grape growing, Larch Hills has varieties that are not generally available in other parts of BC. All wine is made from 100% BC grapes.

Pinot Noir

PRONOUNCED (PEE-NO-NWAHR)

THE PINOT NOIR GRAPE HAS BEEN USED TO MAKE WINE SINCE AT LEAST THE FIRST CENTURY AD. ANCIENT ROMANS CALLED THE GRAPE HELVENACIA MINOR. THE GRAPE IS MOST FAMOUS BECAUSE OF THE WINES PRODUCED IN THE BURGUNDY REGION OF FRANCE.

PINOT NOIR IS KNOWN AS ONE OF THE TOUGHEST GRAPES TO GROW AND TO TURN INTO WINE, YET MANY WINERIES IN BRITISH COLUMBIA HAVE RISEN TO THE CHALLENGE AND SOME GREAT WINE IS THE RESULT. PINOT NOIR HAS NOT REACHED THE POPULARITY OF SOME OTHER REDS BECAUSE ITS OVERALL QUALITY IS GENERALLY A LITTLE MORE INCONSISTENT. HOWEVER, WHEN IT IS DONE RIGHT PINOT NOIR IS MANY WINE LOVERS' FAVOURITE TIPPLE.

PINOT NOIR CAN HAVE MANY DIFFERENT CHARACTERISTICS, BUT SOME COMMON ONES INCLUDE FLAVOURS AND AROMAS OF RASPBERRY, CHERRY, ROSE PETALS, OREGANO AND RHUBARB. THE WINE IS GENERALLY BELIEVED TO BE AT ITS BEST 5-8 YEARS AFTER THE VINTAGE.

THIS WINE IS WONDERFUL WITH A WIDE VARIETY OF FOODS. SOME GREAT PAIRINGS ARE SALMON, TUNA, LAMB, CHICKEN, PORK, SMOKED MEATS, HEARTY STEWS, MUSHROOMS AND DUCK.

Fish & Seafood

Fish, to taste right, must swim three times - in water, in butter and in wine.

Old Polish Proverb

Blue Grouse Poached Salmon with Pinot Gris Sauce

Creamy Seafood in Phyllo Pastry

Carriage House Prawn Linguine

Summerhill's Wild Salmon Stuffed with Red Pepper Cream Cheese

Tuna Steaks with Merlot Butter

House of Rose Salmon Steaks with Red Sauce

Inniskillin's Braised Halibut, Shaved Asparagus and Candied Lemons

Poached Salmon Corn Fritters with Salsa

Prawns in Garlic and Wine

Middle Mountain Mead's Clam Sycee

Gourmet Salmon Burgers

Blossom's Red Snapper in a Pool of Passion Fruit

Chilli Mussels with Vermicelli

Granite Creek's Salmon Wellington in Raspberry Sauce

Almond Crusted Halibut

Whole Roasted Dungeness Crabs

Mt. Boucherie's Mouth-Watering Sundried Tomato Salmon Fillets

Blue Grouse Poached Salmon with Pinot Gris Sauce

Featuring Blue Grouse Pinot Gris

Blue Grouse has produced a magnificent full-bodied Pinot Gris that contains remarkable length in flavour. This wine is perfect for summer sipping and it pairs wonderfully with lamb and game. It is also an ideal accompaniment for salmon and in this dish the fish becomes infused with the Pinot Gris flavour during the poaching process.

Serves 4

INGREDIENTS

1½ cups **Blue Grouse Pinot Gris**

½ cup fish stock

2 shallots, chopped

1 bay leaf

5 whole peppercorns

4 boneless, skinless salmon fillets

(6-8 oz)

½ lemon, sliced

3 tbsp butter

2 garlic cloves, crushed

3 tbsp flour

¼ cup whipping cream

2 tbsp fresh dill, chopped

¼ cup capers

1. In a large pan, combine **Blue Grouse Pinot Gris**, stock, shallots, bay leaf and peppercorns. Bring to a boil then add salmon. Place a lemon slice on each fillet. When liquid returns to a boil, reduce heat immediately, cover and simmer for 10 minutes. If liquid does not cover fish, then it should be carefully turned over halfway through cooking. When fish is cooked, remove with slotted spatula and keep warm. Strain the poaching liquid, setting it aside for later use.

2. Melt butter in a small saucepan over medium heat. Add garlic and sauté for 30 seconds. Stir in the flour. Add reserved poaching liquid, a little at a time, stirring quickly. Simmer for 5-10 minutes then add cream, dill and capers.

3. Serve the salmon drizzled with Pinot Gris sauce, accompanied by basmati rice, steamed asparagus and a glass of **Blue Grouse Pinot Gris**.

Blue Grouse Vineyards

Location: 4365 Blue Grouse Road, Duncan, BC

Telephone: (250) 743-3834

Website and Email: www.bluegrousevineyards.com, info@bluegrousevineyards.com

Wine Shop, Tours and Tastings: Wine shop open Apr-Sep, Wed-Sun 11am-5pm; Oct-Mar, Wed-Sat 11am-5pm.

Getting There: 45km north of Victoria; 7km south of Duncan. From Victoria turn left on Koksilah Road (from Duncan turn right), then immediately left on Hillbank Road and right on Lakeside Road. Second left is Blue Grouse Road. Look for the signs.

Highlights: This is a family-owned/operated vineyard and winery established as one of the founding estate wineries of Vancouver Island in 1989. Visit the elegant wood-panelled wine shop and tasting room. Blue Grouse produces a wide range of award-winning wines and is famous for its unique and distinctive Black Muscat.

Creamy Seafood in Phyllo Pastry

Featuring BC White Wine

The word phyllo is derived from the Greek word for leaf. The paper-thin pastry originated in Turkey during the reign of the Ottomans. It has since been incorporated into our culture and is used in a vast array of wonderful recipes. Here we have golden brown, crispy phyllo pastry wrapped around a creamy seafood combination bursting with juicy shrimp, scallops and crabmeat – all flavoured with rich Gruyère cheese and your favourite BC White Wine.

Serves 4

INGREDIENTS

1½ cups **BC White Wine**

1 tbsp olive oil

2 shallots, chopped

1 garlic clove, crushed

10 oz boneless, skinless salmon fillet, cubed to 1 inch

¼ lb shrimp, cooked, peeled

1 can crabmeat (6 oz)

½ cup Gruyère cheese, grated

3 tbsp butter

3 tbsp flour

8 sheets phyllo pastry

3 tbsp melted butter

1. Heat oil in a small saucepan over medium heat. Sweat the shallots and garlic for 2 minutes then add **BC White Wine**. Bring to a boil then add salmon. Bring back to a boil and then cover and simmer for 3 minutes or until salmon is almost cooked through. Strain poaching liquid and set aside for later use.

2. Combine strained salmon and shallots with shrimp, crab and cheese in a separate bowl.

3. Heat butter in a sauté pan over medium heat. Add flour and combine thoroughly. Slowly add poaching liquid, stirring continuously. Reduce by one-third. Pour sauce over seafood and mix through.

4. Preheat oven to 350°F. Lay out 1 sheet of phyllo pastry and brush with melted butter then place a second sheet on top. Spoon one-quarter of seafood mixture onto the pastry and roll up, being sure to tuck in the ends. Repeat 3 times, using all of the seafood mixture. Brush the top of each phyllo package with the remaining melted butter.

5. Place seafood packages on a greased tray and bake for 20 minutes or until golden brown. Delicious served on garlic mashed potatoes with a glass of **BC White Wine**.

Carriage House Prawn Linguine

Featuring Carriage House Off Dry Kerner

Our flagship off dry white varietal Kerner has been grown in the Okanagan since the mid-1970s. This wine contains a tropical fruit bouquet and flavours. It is excellent with spicy Asian cuisine, white pasta sauces and poultry, or served chilled on its own. A perfect summer sipper – "fruit salad in a glass".

Serves 4

INGREDIENTS

¼ cup **Carriage House Off Dry Kerner**

4 tbsp butter

¼ cup shallots, chopped

1 garlic clove, finely chopped

¼ cup red pepper, chopped

1 cup fresh mushrooms, chopped

1 package cream cheese (10 oz)

½ cup cream

1 tsp fresh dill, chopped, plus some for garnish

3 cups fresh cooked large prawns

1 tsp fresh lemon juice

2 tbsp fresh parsley

fresh linguine

Parmesan cheese to taste

salt and pepper to taste

1. Melt 2 tbsp butter in a large pan over medium heat. Sauté shallots, garlic, red pepper and mushrooms. Reduce heat to low, add cream cheese and cream and stir until the cheese is melted. Add dill, salt, pepper, parsley and **Carriage House Off Dry Kerner**. Stir well and simmer for a few minutes.

2. In a separate pan sauté the prawns with 1 tbsp of butter and fresh lemon juice. Drain and keep warm.

3. Cook the pasta as directed on the package. Toss the drained linguine with 1 tbsp butter and Parmesan cheese.

4. Add prawns and parsley to the sauce, reserving a few prawns for garnish and serve over the linguine. Garnish with dill, reserved prawns and Parmesan cheese. Accompany with a glass of **Carriage House Off Dry Kerner**.

Carriage House Wines

Location: 32764 Black Sage Road, Oliver, BC

Telephone: (250) 498-8818

Website and Email: www.carriagehousewines.ca, wineinfo@carriagehousewines.ca

Wine Shop, Tours and Tastings: Wine shop is open for sales and tastings from Easter to Nov 11, daily 10am-6pm. Any other time by appointment.

Getting There: Off of Highway 97 South. 7km south of Oliver. Watch for "Wine Route" signs on the highway. Well signposted.

Highlights: This is a small family-owned and operated winery, selling award-winning handcrafted wines that are not readily available elsewhere.

Kerner

Wohlauf! Noch getrunken den funkelnden Wein!

This is the start of a poem by Justus Andreas Christian Kerner, a German poet of the 1800s. It is about drinking sparkling wine with friends. Perhaps it is this type of prose that encouraged someone at the Weinsberg Institute of Oenology and Viticulture to name a new variety of grape after the poet.

The Kerner grape was created in 1969 and is a cross between Riesling and Trollinger. This variety of grape is quite hardy and frost resistant. The grapes actually look very similar to the parent Trollinger grapes but are a bit smaller and they do not have the red colouring.

The grape made its way to Canada early in its existence. It was planted in the Okanagan during the mid-1970s by George and Trudy Heiss of Gray Monk on the advice of German wine expert Dr Helmut Becker of the Geisenheim Institute.

Kerner is a versatile wine that is reminiscent of Riesling, although it is often a little spicier. Kerner is wonderful paired with fish and seafood, pork, ham, spicy cheese and creamy pasta.

Summerhill's Wild Salmon Stuffed with Red Pepper Cream Cheese

Featuring Summerhill Pinot Blanc

Summerhill's most food friendly wine, this classic Alsatian variety was crafted using 100% certified organic grapes. The aromas in the 2002 Pinot Blanc are all fresh fruits: Granny Smith apples, Bartlett pears and a hint of lime. Crisp, bright acidity greets the tongue announcing flavours of citrus, green apples and lemongrass, with a slight lingering sweetness on the finish.

Serves 1

INGREDIENTS

¼-½ cup **Summerhill Pinot Blanc**

3 tbsp roasted red pepper, minced

2 tbsp cream cheese

1 salmon fillet (6oz)

1 tbsp olive oil

salt and pepper to taste

1. Blend the roasted red pepper into the cream cheese.

2. Slice through the salmon fillet from the side, creating an envelope. Add cream cheese filling to the inside of the salmon fillet. Season the salmon fillet with salt and pepper.

3. Heat oil over medium heat in a sauté pan. Add salmon fillet, browning on both sides, cooking through to the centre.

4. Remove salmon fillet and deglaze the pan with **Summerhill Pinot Blanc**, using a wooden spoon to scrape up the bits from the bottom of the pan. Pour the sauce over the fillet and serve immediately with a glass of **Summerhill Pinot Blanc**.

Summerhill Pyramid Winery

Location: 4870 Chute Lake Road, Kelowna, BC

Telephone/Fax: 1 (800) 667-3538 / (250) 764-2598

Website and Email: www.summerhill.bc.ca, info@summerhill.bc.ca

Wine Shop, Tours and Tastings: Summerhill's wine shop is open year-round, 9am-9pm daily, serving free tastings of vibrant award-winning wines. The famous sparkling winemaking tours and pyramid tours run daily at noon, 1pm, 2pm, 3pm and 4pm.

Getting There: Summerhill is located 15 minutes from downtown Kelowna. Go south on Pandosy off of Highway 97 and follow the "Wine Route" signs.

Highlights: Summerhill is Canada's largest certified organic vineyard. It has an authentic Pyramid Wine Cellar. You can dine in style at Forster's Sunset Bistro, which has a breathtaking view overlooking Okanagan Lake.

Summerhill's Wild Salmon Stuffed with Red Pepper Cream Cheese. Photo courtesy of Summerhill Pyramid Winery

ABOUT SUMMERHILL PYRAMID WINERY

The Summerhill Pyramid Vineyard comprises over 65 acres, of which approximately 45 are planted. The organically-grown grape varieties include Riesling, Chardonnay, Pinot Noir, Gewürztraminer, Ehrenfelser and Pinot Meunier. They are flourishing here in the northernmost desert viticulture region of the world.

Summerhill is a certified organic vineyard, using no herbicides, pesticides, or chemical fertilizers in the soil. Glacier rock dust is added to provide trace minerals. Remineralized soils are proving to produce more flavourful, healthier foods wherever they are used.

At Summerhill, wine is aged in a 3249 square foot replica of the Great Pyramid. This four-storey high structure must be seen to be believed. Blind taste tests have shown that consumers actually prefer pyramid-aged wines. But you don't have to take our word for it, come and test this theory for yourself.

Tuna Steaks with Merlot Butter

Featuring BC Merlot

Merlot is a wine that really compliments the beef-like characteristics of tuna. It is interesting to note that in the mid-1970s a large tuna would be sold for about a penny a pound and would likely be turned into cat food. Today the same fish could sell for up to $50 a pound to be eaten as sushi! This mouth-watering recipe will leave you wishing you could turn back the clock.

Serves 4

INGREDIENTS

½ cup **BC Merlot**

4 tbsp soy sauce

2 tbsp pure sesame oil

¼ cup dry sherry

4 tuna steaks (6-8 oz)

3 tsp lemon juice

$1/3$ cup butter, cut into chunks

1 tbsp ginger, minced

2 tbsp olive oil

1. In a non-metallic bowl, combine soy sauce, sesame oil and sherry. Mix well and add tuna steaks to the bowl, covering them with the mixture. Cover and refrigerate for 1 hour, turning them over every 15 minutes.

2. Mix **BC Merlot** with lemon juice in a non-aluminium saucepan over medium heat. Reduce mixture to one-third. Lower the heat, add the ginger and whisk in butter chunks one by one.

3. Remove tuna from the marinade. Tuna can be cooked in a pan over medium-high heat with olive oil or on a barbeque. Either way, cook for 3 minutes on each side for medium rare or longer for medium or well-done.

4. Cover the steaks in the merlot butter sauce before serving. Accompany with a glass of **BC Merlot**.

House of Rose Salmon Steaks with Red Sauce

Featuring House of Rose Merlot

Our award-winning Merlot has a nose of soft berry and flavours of bell pepper, red currant, cherry and spice. Lightly oaked, it is excellent with fish or seafood, creamy pastas or red meat.

Serves 4

INGREDIENTS

¼ cup **House of Rose Merlot**	6 tbsp butter
4 salmon steaks (6 oz)	1½ cups mushrooms
¼ cup flour	1 tbsp sugar
¼ tsp salt and pepper	1 cup heavy cream

1. Dry steaks well with paper towels. Reserving 1 tbsp flour for later use, coat the salmon steaks with a mixture of flour, salt and pepper. Melt 2 tbsp butter in skillet over medium heat and sauté steaks for 3-4 minutes, until browned on each side. Remove from the skillet, arrange on a serving platter and keep warm.

2. Add 2 tbsp of butter to the skillet and add mushrooms. Sauté until tender. Pile a few mushrooms on top of each steak.

3. In a separate small saucepan over medium heat, combine the remaining butter and reserved flour together to form a roux. Set aside.

4. Deglaze the skillet with **House of Rose Merlot** and simmer until liquid is reduced to about 2 tbsp. Dissolve the sugar into the wine and add the cream. Bring almost to a boil. Lift off the heat and add the roux, a little at a time, stirring well. Return to the heat and simmer for 2 minutes. Spoon the sauce over the steaks and serve. Accompany with a glass of **House of Rose Merlot**.

House of Rose Winery

Location: 2270 Garner Road, Kelowna, BC

Telephone/Fax: (250) 765-0802 / (250) 765-7762

Website and Email: www.winegrowers.bc.ca, arose@shuswap.net

Wine Shop, Tours and Tastings: Open every day except Christmas for tours and tastings. Experience one of the best tours in the valley, taste our award-winning wine and enjoy the family atmosphere.

Getting There: From Highway 97, turn onto Highway 33. Travel 6km up Highway 33 to our sign. Turn right and follow Garner Road for 2km.

Highlights: The multi award-winning winter wines are a delectable combination of icewine and grapes picked late in the fall.

Inniskillin's Braised Halibut, Shaved Asparagus and Candied Lemons

Featuring Inniskillin Okanagan Chardonnay Reserve

The grapes for this Chardonnay were sourced from select vineyard sites in the Okanagan Valley. Characterised with mild citrus and vanilla aromas, this medium-bodied Chardonnay's honey and apple flavours nicely compliment the braised halibut and candied lemons.

Serves 6

INGREDIENTS

1½ cups **Inniskillin Okanagan Chardonnay Reserve**

2 lemons

¾ cup sugar

2 lbs halibut

1 tbsp butter, melted

2 cups fish stock

7 tbsp cold butter, cut in chunks

2 shallots, minced

2 bunches asparagus

thick end of lemongrass (2 inches), thinly sliced

1 tbsp whipping cream

salt and pepper to taste

1. Preheat oven to 350°F. Wash lemons and cut into thin slices. Place slices in a pan with sugar and enough water to cover. Simmer gently until lemons are covered with reduced syrup. Remove slices to cool.

2. Place halibut in an ovenproof skillet and brush with melted butter. Pour 1 cup of fish stock and 1 cup of **Inniskillin Okanagan Chardonnay Reserve** over the halibut, seasoning lightly with salt and pepper. Bring the halibut to a simmer on the stovetop. As soon as it simmers transfer it to the oven for 15 minutes, or until done (springy to touch). Remove from the oven and keep warm in foil. Pour cooking liquid into a small pan and reduce to 1 tbsp of liquid.

3. To prepare the sauce, melt 1 tsp of butter in saucepan. Add shallots and sweat until translucent. Add remaining **Inniskillin Okanagan Chardonnay Reserve** and reduce until almost all of the liquid is gone.

Inniskillin Okanagan Vineyards

Location: Road 11, Oliver, BC

Telephone: (250) 498-6663

Website: www.inniskillin.com, info@inniskillin.com

Wine Shop, Tours and Tastings: The Wine Boutique is open Nov-Apr, Monday to Friday 10am-3pm. Extended summer hours May–Oct, daily 10am-5pm. Tours available May-Oct at 11am and 3pm daily.

Getting There: From Osoyoos, at the Highway 97 and Highway 3 junction, head north on Highway 97. Turn left onto Road 11 West (123rd St) and travel 1km to the winery entrance. From Penticton travel south on Highway 97 to the south of Oliver and turn right on Road 11 West.

Highlights: Tour the winery and Dark Horse Estate Vineyard to experience all the fine pleasures the Okanagan has to offer.

The beautiful Inniskillin Okanagan vineyards. Photo courtesy of Inniskillin Okanagan.

4. Trim asparagus, cut off tips and shave stalks with a vegetable peeler. Season tips with salt and pepper and steam them in a steamer until almost done. Add shavings for a few minutes and then remove and keep warm.

5. Continue with the sauce by adding remaining fish stock and lemongrass. Reduce by half then add reduced liquid from halibut and whisk in cold butter chunk by chunk. Pass mixture through a sieve and return to stovetop. Add lemons from step 1 and cream, season and remove from heat.

6. Serve halibut on a bed of asparagus tips, with the asparagus shavings on top, and surround with the lemon emulsion. Accompany with a glass of **Inniskillin Okanagan Chardonnay Reserve**.

Inniskillin Okanagan Vineyards

Inniskillin Okanagan Vineyards was originally established in 1994 by Donald Ziraldo as a partnership between Inniskillin Wines and the Osoyoos Indian Band. The winery's first vintage was in 1994, with an annual production of 3300 cases. In 1996 Inniskillin Okanagan found its own home, with the purchase of an existing winery, formerly named Okanagan Vineyards. Since then, Inniskillin Okanagan Vineyards has been producing premium award-winning VQA wines, including Chardonnay, Pinot Noir, Meritage, Riesling and Vidal Icewine, as well as Canada's first Zinfandel.

At Inniskillin Okanagan Vineyards you can taste some of Canada's great wines in the beautiful setting of the South Okanagan Valley. Come visit the winery, take a tour of our beautiful Dark Horse Estate Vineyard and shop for your favourite Inniskillin Okanagan wines in our boutique.

After you have completed your winery tour, stay in the area to take advantage of some of the other great seasonal activities including camping, hiking, golf, skiing and much more.

Poached Salmon Corn Fritters with Salsa

Featuring BC White Wine

It is no secret that British Columbia produces some of the best corn in the world. If you are around Chilliwack during September why not visit the Corn Maze for a fun way to get lost. Here you can use some of this wonderful produce to create tasty salmon fritters and a tangy corn salsa.

Serves 4

INGREDIENTS

1½ cups **BC White Wine**

1 lb boneless, skinless salmon fillets

2 cups fresh corn kernels

½ cup green onions, chopped

½ cup celery, chopped

1 cup red pepper, chopped

½ cup mayonnaise (see page 37)

1 tsp Dijon mustard

1 egg

4 tbsp fresh basil, chopped

½ cup breadcrumbs

1 large tomato, chopped

½ cup red onion, chopped

2 garlic cloves, crushed

1 lime, juiced

1 tbsp olive oil

salt and pepper to taste

1. Place **BC White Wine** in a pan over high heat and bring to a boil. As soon as it boils add salmon, cover and simmer for 5-10 minutes. If wine does not cover the fish you will have to flip it over midway. When fish flakes apart with a fork it is done.

2. In a large bowl combine poached fish with 1 cup of corn, green onions, celery, half of the red pepper, mayonnaise, mustard, egg, 2 tbsp basil and half of the breadcrumbs. Using your hands, mix together and form into patties. Use remaining breadcrumbs to coat the patties. Cover and refrigerate for 2-3 hours.

3. Place remaining corn on a baking sheet under the broiler for 5-7 minutes or until partially cooked. In a separate bowl mix the partially cooked corn with remaining red pepper, tomato, red onion, garlic, remaining basil and lime juice. Mix well and refrigerate until needed.

4. After patties have been refrigerated, heat olive oil in a frying pan over medium-low heat. Fry the patties until they are golden brown and then serve with the salsa.

Opposite: Inniskillin's Braised Halibut with Shaved Asparagus and Candied Lemons (Pg 78) Photo: Gary Faessler

Prawns in Garlic and Wine

Featuring BC White Wine

Sometimes recipes seem too simple. That is the case with this easy to prepare dish. Juicy West Coast prawns, garlic, wine, shallots and butter make up some the finer things in life. This dish also makes a great appetizer for 4.

Serves 2

INGREDIENTS

¼ cup **BC White Wine**

1 lb large raw prawns, peeled and de-veined

2 tbsp flour

4 tbsp butter

2 garlic cloves, crushed

1 tbsp shallots, chopped

2 tbsp fresh lemon juice

2 tbsp fresh parsley, chopped for garnish

1. Coat the prawns lightly with flour, dusting off any excess.

2. Heat 3 tbsp of butter in a frying pan over medium heat. Add garlic and shallots and sauté for 30 seconds. Add the prawns lightly searing on one side before turning. When the prawns are lightly seared on both sides add the **BC White Wine** and lemon juice.

3. Move the prawns around in the pan to ensure they are coated in the wine. The prawns will turn opaque when they are cooked. Let the liquid reduce a little before removing from the heat.

4. Stir though the remaining butter. Serve sprinkled with chopped parsley and a glass of **BC White Wine**. We told you it was good!

Opposite: Dining on the terrace at Mission Hill Family Estate Winery
Photo: Brian Sprout courtesy of Mission Hill Family Estate Winery

Middle Mountain Mead's Clam Sycee

Featuring Middle Mountain Tea Mead

There are few wine pairings that really work to bring out the best in Asian food. This blend of honey wine with green and black tea is an exception. It is delicious on its own, but when used in cooking it adds a special Asian flavour. The clamshells look like "sycee", silver ingots used as money in ancient China. Sycee is traditionally served during the Chinese New Year.

Serves 4

INGREDIENTS

½ cup **Middle Mountain Tea Mead**

2 dozen clams, scrubbed and rinsed

¾ lb ground pork

2 tbsp sherry

2 tbsp soy sauce

2 tbsp cornstarch

2 tbsp water

2 tbsp sesame oil

2 tsp olive oil

1 slice ginger

1 green onion, cut diagonally in thirds

¾ cup chicken broth or stock

1 tbsp oyster sauce

1 tsp sugar

salt to taste

1. Add the clams to boiling water. As soon as they open remove them with a slotted spoon. Remove the meat from the clams, setting the shells aside for later. Mince the clam meat and combine with the ground pork. Stir in 1 tbsp sherry, 1 tbsp soy sauce, 1 tbsp cornstarch and salt. Stuff this mixture into the clamshells.

2. Mix remaining cornstarch with water to form a paste. Rub the paste over the ground meat. Any extra cornstarch paste will be added to the sauce later. Heat a wok or large frying pan over medium heat. Add sesame oil and carefully place the clams in the wok, meat side down and stir fry until golden. Remove and set aside to drain.

3. In wok combine olive oil, **Middle Mountain Tea Mead**, remaining sherry and soy sauce, ginger, green onion, chicken broth, oyster sauce and sugar. Add clams back to the wok and simmer covered for about 20 minutes. Add any remaining cornstarch/water paste, stirring quickly to thicken. Serve hot, over rice if desired. Enjoy with a glass of **Middle Mountain Tea Mead**.

Middle Mountain Mead

Location: 3505 Euston Road, Hornby Island, BC

Telephone: (250) 335-1392

Website and Email: www.middlemountainmead.com, info@middlemountainmead.com

Wine Shop, Tours and Tastings: Open Wed-Sat 1pm-5pm, summer only; or by appointment. Check the website for current information.

Getting There: Hornby Island is 2 ferry rides from Vancouver Island's Buckley Bay, it is located 1 hour north of Nanaimo; 20 minutes south of Courtney.

Highlights: Middle Mountain Mead is an artisan honey winery set in acres of gardens, with magnificent water and mountain views.

Mead

PRONOUNCED (MEED)

MEAD SEEMS TO HAVE BEEN AROUND FOR A VERY LONG TIME. LEGEND HAS IT THAT OLD KING MIDAS WAS A MEAD DRINKER; THE VIKINGS' NORSE GODS WERE ALSO FOND OF IMBIBING THE INTOXICATING NECTAR IN VALHALLA. TODAY, PERHAPS AIDED BY MOVIES SUCH AS THE LORD OF THE RINGS, MEAD IS EXPERIENCING A RESURGENCE.

MEAD IS ACTUALLY A FERMENTED ALCOHOLIC BEVERAGE MADE OF HONEY, WATER AND YEAST. IT IS ESSENTIALLY A HONEY WINE. IT IS RELATIVELY NEW TO BRITISH COLUMBIA AND THE FIRST MEADERY ESTABLISHED HERE WAS THE TUGWELL CREEK HONEY FARM AND MEADERY IN SOOKE ON VANCOUVER ISLAND.

IF YOU HAVE NEVER TRIED MEAD (AND MOST PEOPLE HAVE NOT) IT IS WELL WORTH THE TRIP TO ONE OF THE MEADERIES TO SAMPLE SOME; OTHERWISE LOOK FOR IT IN YOUR LOCAL LIQUOR STORE OR BEER AND WINE STORE.

MEAD CAN BE PAIRED SUCCESSFULLY WITH MANY TYPES OF FOODS, BUT WITH SO MANY TYPES OF MEAD IT IS HARD TO GENERALISE. SOME OF THE MEADS WE HAVE TRIED PAIRED WELL WITH SPICY DISHES, SHELLFISH AND ASIAN DISHES. MEAD ALSO GOES WELL WITH DESSERT AND SOME VARIETIES COULD EVEN BE CONSUMED AS A DESSERT ON THEIR OWN.

Gourmet Salmon Burgers

Featuring BC White Wine

This recipe turns burgers into a gourmet treat. These will please both burger lovers and seafood lovers. It is a great way to sample some of British Columbia's world famous West Coast wild salmon.

Serves 8-10

INGREDIENTS

1 cup **BC White Wine**

¼ cup olive oil

4 large shallots, chopped

½ cup lemon juice

1 jar of capers (3-4 oz)

2 lbs boneless, skinless salmon fillets

3 cups breadcrumbs

3 eggs, beaten

¼ cup dill, chopped

1 tsp salt

½ tsp black pepper

8–10 burger buns

your favourite burger toppings (tomato, lettuce, mayonnaise, cheese, pickles, onions, etc.)

1. Heat 1 tbsp of oil in a frying pan over medium heat. Add shallots and sauté for 5 minutes. Add **BC White Wine**, lemon juice and capers. Increase heat to medium-high and cook an additional 8-10 minutes, reducing until the liquid is almost gone. Remove from heat, transfer to a bowl, cover and refrigerate for 1-2 hours.

2. Remove any small bones from the salmon fillets. Transfer salmon fillets into a food processor and pulse until salmon is coarsely ground.

3. Add ground salmon, breadcrumbs, dill, eggs, salt and pepper to the shallot mixture. Mix well and form into 8-10 equally sized patties. Lay patties on a tray, cover and refrigerate for 1-2 hours.

4. Heat remaining olive oil in a large skillet over medium-high heat. Add salmon patties a few at a time and cook for 2-3 minutes on each side.

5. Serve the salmon burgers on buns, along with all of your favourite toppings.

Blossom's Red Snapper in a Pool of Passion Fruit

Featuring Blossom's Eros Passion Fruit Wine

In Greek mythology, Eros was the God in charge of passionate and physical love as well as fertility. His name is the base of the word "erotic". To make this wine we carefully carve out the pulp and seeds inside the passion fruit. Then we use a longer, traditional winemaking process resulting in an exotic passion fruit wine. Open this wine and you will fall passionately in love.

Serves 4

INGREDIENTS

1 cup **Blossom's Eros Passion Fruit Wine**

2 tbsp olive oil

1 shallot, finely chopped

$1/_3$ cup cold butter, cubed

4 boneless, skinless red snapper fillets (6-8 oz)

¼ cup flour

salt and pepper to taste

1. In a small saucepan heat ½ tbsp of olive oil and sauté shallot until softened. Add ¾ cup **Blossom's Eros Passion Fruit Wine** and reduce by half. Remove from the heat and continue stirring, adding butter, bit by bit, until all is whisked in. Cover and set aside.

2. Season the fish with salt and pepper and then coat one side in flour. Heat 1½ tbsp of oil over medium heat. When oil is hot, add fish, flour-side down and fry until fish is golden brown. Turn fish over, add remaining **Blossom's Eros Passion Fruit Wine** and cook for 1-2 minutes before removing from heat.

3. Make a pool of passion fruit sauce in the middle of each plate and place snapper fillet in the centre. This meal is absolutely divine. Serve with a glass of **Blossom's Eros Passion Fruit Wine**.

Blossom Winery

Location: 5491 Minoru Boulevard, Richmond, BC

Telephone/Fax: (604) 232-9839 / (604) 232-9836

Website and Email: www.blossomwinery.com, info@blossomwinery.com

Wine Shop, Tours and Tastings: Free tasting at the winery. Open Mon-Fri 10am-6pm; Sat 11am-6pm. For tours please call to make an appointment.

Getting There: Located in Richmond on Minoru Boulevard between Alderbridge Way (Highway 91) and Westminster Highway. Only 20 minutes from Vancouver.

Highlights: Blossom winery produces a unique and dynamic selection of wines to excite every palate and compliment every portfolio. Creations include the delectable Raspberry Wine, Passion Fruit Wine and a variety of premium grade reds and whites befitting any dining occasion.

Chilli Mussels with Vermicelli

Featuring BC Gewürztraminer

There are not many wines that can hold up to a spicy dish as well as Gewürztraminer. Here the spicy wine also compliments the tender sweet meat of the mussels. Mussels are a cost effective, easy way to create a 5-star meal in the comfort of your own home.

Serves 4

INGREDIENTS

1 cup **BC Gewürztraminer**

2 lbs fresh live mussels

1 stalk lemon grass

1 package vermicelli rice noodles (6oz)

1 tbsp olive oil

2 shallots, chopped

3 garlic cloves, crushed

1 piece of ginger, sliced (1 inch)

2 small red chillies, chopped

¾ cup fish stock (or water)

¼ cup fresh cilantro, chopped for garnish

1. Scrub mussels well under cold running water, removing the beards. Remove and discard any mussels that are not closed tightly.

2. Cut the lemongrass into 1 inch pieces, splitting each section in half lengthwise and set aside. Place vermicelli noodles in hot water for 3-5 minutes or until tender. Drain and set aside.

3. Heat oil in a large pan over medium heat. Sauté shallots, garlic and ginger for 2 minutes. Add **BC Gewürztraminer**, lemongrass, chilli and mussels. Cover and steam for 1 minute. Add stock and continue steaming for 2-3 minutes, until mussels are open. Discard any unopened mussels.

4. Place noodles in individual serving bowls and cover with broth and mussels. Garnish with cilantro and serve with a glass of **BC Gewürztraminer**.

Chef's Tip

All the mussels should be closed before you begin cooking. If by gently tapping the mussel shell on a counter top it does not close, discard it. Likewise, you should not cook with any mussels with broken or damaged shells.

Ehrenfelser

PRONOUNCED (AIR-EN—FELTS-ER)

THE EHRENFELSER GRAPE VARIETY WAS CREATED IN 1929 BY THE GEISENHEIM INSTITUTE IN GERMANY. THE NAME COMES FROM SCHLOSS EHRENFELS, A ONCE-GREAT CASTLE SITTING UPON THE RHINE RIVER. THE CASTLE WAS BUILT IN THE 13TH CENTURY BUT WAS DESTROYED IN THE LATE 1600S. THE MAJESTIC RUINS INSPIRED SOMEONE AT THE INSTITUTE TO ENSURE THAT THE LEGACY OF THE CASTLE LIVES ON TODAY.

THE GEISENHEIM INSTITUTE ALSO PLAYED A ROLE IN BRINGING THE GRAPE TO BRITISH COLUMBIA. WALTER GEHRINGER, OF GEHRINGER BROTHERS WINERY, IS A GRADUATE OF THE INSTITUTE AND IN THE LATE 1970S IT WAS HIS RECOMMENDATION THAT BROUGHT THE VARIETY HERE. TODAY EHRENFELSER IS MORE FAMOUS IN BRITISH COLUMBIA THAN JUST ABOUT ANYWHERE ELSE IN THE WORLD.

THE GRAPE, WHICH RIPENS EARLIER THAN RIESLING, HAS FLOWERY AROMAS AND IS USUALLY A LITTLE SWEET. THESE WINES ARE NOT RECOMMENDED FOR CELLARING, ALTHOUGH THEY WILL CERTAINLY KEEP FOR A FEW YEARS.

IN BRITISH COLUMBIA EHRENFELSER IS USED TO CREATE BOTH TABLE AND DESSERT WINES. IT MAKES A GREAT ACCOMPANIMENT TO SPICY INDIAN FOOD BUT ALSO GOES WELL WITH LIGHT, SIMPLE FARE.

Granite Creek's Salmon Wellington in Raspberry Sauce

Featuring Granite Creek Ehrenfelser

This recipe is an adaptation of a recipe created by Chef Eric Thomas of The Inn at Kristofer's. The Ehrenfelser wine serves up fragrant pineapple and clove aromas and juicy cocktail flavours. It has lively acids and zing, while orange peel and spice notes round out the finish. Sip it on its own or serve with fruit and cheese.

Serves 6

INGREDIENTS

8 oz cooked shrimp, shelled	¼ cup whipping cream
4 oz cream cheese	2 pkgs frozen puff pastry, thawed
2 tbsp fresh basil, chopped	6 boneless, skinless salmon fillets
3 garlic cloves, minced	(6-8 oz)
2 large eggs	salt and pepper to taste

1. Place shrimp in a food processor and pulse, chopping coarsely. Add cream cheese, basil, garlic, salt and pepper. Pulse to combine. You now have shrimp mousse. Transfer it to a bowl and refrigerate.

2. In a small bowl combine the eggs and cream. Lay a piece of parchment paper on a baking sheet and set aside. Place 1 package of puff pastry on a lightly floured board. Use a rolling pin and roll out all sides. Cut pastry into 3 equal rectangular pieces. Repeat with the second package of puff pastry.

3. Lay a piece of salmon in the middle of each pastry piece. Carefully spread one-sixth of the mousse mix on top of each piece of salmon. Flip salmon pieces over so that the mouse is now against the pastry. Using a pastry brush, coat the exposed sides of pastry with the egg mixture. Bring the long sides of the pastry rectangle up around the salmon so that they overlap and press ends gently to adhere. Trim off excess pastry. Bring the short ends of the pastry up and press to adhere.

4. Place the salmon package on the prepared, parchment-lined baking sheet with the seam side down and the mousse side up. Brush the top and sides of the pastry with egg mixture. Continue this process with the remaining salmon packages. Save leftover pastry to use as decorations – try making freeform leaves or use cookie cutters. Brush your decorations with egg mixture, place on top of the Wellingtons and refrigerate for 15 minutes.

5. Preheat oven to 375°F. After salmon has been refrigerated, place in oven for 25-30 minutes, or until internal temperature reaches 140°F. Remove the Wellingtons and allow them to rest for 5 minutes.

6. When ready to serve, slice the Wellington in half on a horizontal angle. Place one piece on top of the other at an angle. Serve on a pool of raspberry sauce (next page) with a few stir-fried vegetables. Accompany this dish with a glass of **Granite Creek Ehrenfelser**.

Raspberry Sauce

INGREDIENTS

1½ cups **Granite Creek Ehrenfelser**

2 cups frozen unsweetened raspberries

½ cup extra fine sugar (or to taste)

½ cup balsamic vinegar

2 shallots, chopped

3 garlic cloves, chopped

2 tbsp lemon juice

¾ cup apple juice

1 tbsp cornstarch

3 tbsp water

1. Thaw berries. Place in a food processor and pulse. Add sugar to taste and pulse to combine. Strain the sauce to remove seeds and store in refrigerator.

2. In a saucepan over medium heat combine **Granite Creek Ehrenfelser**, vinegar, shallots, garlic and lemon juice. Simmer for about 20 minutes, until mixture is reduced by half. Add the raspberry purée and the apple juice. Simmer for 15 minutes.

3. In a small bowl combine cornstarch with water and add it to the mixture a little at a time until the sauce thickens. This sauce can be made ahead of time and refrigerated. Reheat when ready to use.

Granite Creek Estate Wines

Location: 2302 Skimikin Road, Tappen, BC

Telephone/Fax: (250) 835-0049 / (250) 835-0048

Website: www.granitecreek.ca

Wine Shop, Tours and Tastings: Open Apr, May, Jun, Oct, daily noon-5pm; Jul-Sep, daily 10am-5pm; Nov 1-Mar 31 by appointment.

Getting There: Located just 5 minutes west of Salmon Arm. Turn off the Trans-Canada Highway onto Tappen Valley Road and follow the signs for 5km to the winery.

Highlights: This is a family-owned vineyard and winery. It is one of Canada's most northerly vineyards, slightly north in latitude of the famed German wine region of Rheingau.

Almond Crusted Halibut

Featuring BC White Wine

Yes, it is really this simple! It seems too good to be true and so will the results. Of course fresh halibut is the key and make sure you use a wine that you really like as the flavour will carry right through. The best tasting fillets comes from halibut that are 15-30 lbs. Fish of this size are often referred to as 'chicken of the sea'. British Columbia offers some of the best halibut fishing in the world.

Serves 4

INGREDIENTS

¾ cup **BC White Wine**

¾ cup sliced almonds

4 skinless halibut fillets (6-8 oz)

¼ cup flour

2 eggs, beaten

3 tbsp butter

salt and pepper to taste

1. Place a dry pan over medium heat and add sliced almonds. Mix well until almonds are toasty and aromatic. Remove from heat and set aside.

2. Season fish to taste with salt and pepper. Dust the halibut fillets with flour and then dip them in the beaten egg. Coat the fillets entirely with the toasted almonds.

3. Melt butter in a large sauté pan over medium-high heat. Add the **BC White Wine** until it begins to bubble and then add fish to the pan. Cook for approximately 5 minutes on each side or until flesh is opaque and it breaks apart with a fork.

4. Serve immediately, topped with any remaining sauce from the pan. This is delicious served with a leafy salad.

Whole Roasted Dungeness Crabs

Featuring BC White Wine

Dungeness crabs are available in British Columbia year-round although most are caught between the months of May and October. The Dungeness crab is one of 35 crab species living in the Pacific waters off the BC coast. These crabs have been harvested by Canada's Aboriginal population for thousands of years.

Serves 2

INGREDIENTS

¼ cup **BC White Wine**

6 garlic cloves

2 tbsp + 1 tsp olive oil

2 live Dungeness crabs (2 lbs each)

2 shallots, chopped

½ sprig rosemary, chopped

¼ cup butter

1 tbsp garlic salt

1. Preheat oven to 425°F. Place garlic cloves in a small baking dish and cover with 1 tsp olive oil. Roast for 30 minutes until soft. Set aside.

2. Plunge the crabs into a large pot of boiling water for about 10 minutes, until they are bright red. Remove from the boiling water and immerse them in iced cold water for 3-4 minutes.

3. Preheat oven to 325°F. To remove the shell, hold the crab with your left hand. Use your right hand to grip the shell. Place your thumb under the shell at the centre back of the crab and pull off the shell. (try and keep it in one piece). Wash and dry the shell and set aside for later. You will now see the leaf-gills or dead man's fingers. Gently scrape them away. Wash away the guts of the crab under running water and wipe clean. Lay the cleaned crabs in a baking dish and set aside.

4. Heat 1 tbsp oil in a saucepan over medium heat. Sauté the shallot with the rosemary for 5 minutes. Add the **BC White Wine**, butter and garlic salt and stir well. Bring to a simmer and reduce heat to low and simmer for 10 minutes.

5. Remove butter mixture from the heat. and strain. Using a fork or whisk, mix in the roasted garlic. Pour the mixture over the crabs in the baking dish reserving a little for a dipping sauce.

6. Bake crabs for 15-20 minutes. Arrange crabs on a serving dish and place the empty head shells back on top. Coat the shell with extra olive oil to give it a shine. Serve immediately with the extra garlic butter for dipping.

Mt. Boucherie's Mouth-Watering Sundried Tomato Salmon Fillets

Featuring Mt. Boucherie Semillon

The 2003 Mt. Boucherie Semillon displays aromas and flavours of dried apricot, guava, rose petal, tangerine and a slight herbal note, with rich oily mouth feel and a crisp finish. All of our wines are carefully crafted from only the finest British Columbia estate–grown grapes and proudly bear the VQA seal of quality. A true family-owned and operated affair, our aim is to produce the finest white wines, red wines and dessert wines for every palate.

Serves 4

INGREDIENTS

¾ cup **Mt. Boucherie Semillon**

1 cup parsley

½ cup sundried tomatoes, in oil

4 garlic cloves

4 boneless, skinless salmon fillets

salt and pepper to taste

1. Combine parsley, sundried tomatoes and garlic in a food processor for 15 seconds. Stop before it becomes a paste. If no food processor is available, finely chop all ingredients and combine in a bowl.

2. Transfer mixed ingredients to a non-metallic bowl and add **Mt. Boucherie Semillon**, salt and pepper. Place fish fillets in the bowl and cover with the marinade. Refrigerate for 1 hour.

3. Just before removing the salmon from the refrigerator, preheat oven to 400°F or fire up the barbeque. Transfer fillets, well-covered by the marinade, to a sheet of aluminium foil. If there is extra marinade, spoon over top of each fillet. Place aluminium sheets topped with fillets on a baking sheet and put in the oven (or directly on the barbeque) for 12-15 minutes, or until flesh flakes with a fork.

4. Serve fish with wild rice or pearl couscous, steamed asparagus and a glass of **Mt. Boucherie Semillon**.

Mt. Boucherie Estate Winery

Location: 829 Douglas Road, Kelowna, BC

Telephone/Fax: (250) 769-8803 / (250) 769-9330

Website and Email: www.mtboucherie.bc.ca, sales@mtboucherie.bc.ca

Wine Shop, Tours and Tastings: Wine shop is open daily for tastings. Summer 10am-6pm; winter 11am-5pm.

Getting There: 10 minutes from downtown Kelowna. Take Highway 97 west across the floating bridge. Turn left at Boucherie Road traffic lights, follow and turn left again onto Douglas Road.

Highlights: Visit the wine shop and gift boutique. Partake in daily wine tasting or enjoy a bottle of your favourite vintage in the licensed picnic area.

Semillon

Pronounced (seh-mee-yon)

Semillon is the white grape that is most famous when blended with the Sauvignon Blanc grape to create the dry wines of Bordeaux. It is also commonly blended with Chardonnay, but is an outstanding wine on its own. As well as being a table wine, it can be used to make wonderful dessert wines when affected by Botrytis cinerea, also called noble rot.

This variety of grape does well all over the world with great wines coming from countries as diverse as Israel, Portugal, Tunisia, Australia, Argentina and South Africa. In South Africa it has been prominent since the early 1800s. It is believed that at one time Semillon was the world's most commonly grown grape.

This grape ripens earlier than many other varieties, which makes it less susceptible to frosts. The grapes are thick-skinned and are generally a dark shade of yellow, although sometimes they gain a slight tinge of pink. They grow very well in British Columbia and the wine seems to be gaining popularity.

Semillon, like Riesling, develops very well in the bottle and can be easily cellared for 5 years with great results. After aging, hazelnut characteristics are common. When consumed young, the wine has a figgy, sometimes floral flavour. This wine pairs very well with risotto, pilaf and other grain dishes, fish and seafood.

Poultry

When I demanded of my friend what viands he preferred,
He quoth, "A large cold bottle, and a small hot bird!"

Eugene Field 1850 – 1895

Florentine Chicken

Pinot Noir Chicken with Grapes

Free-Range Turkey in White Wine

Stuffed Chicken Breast with White Wine Sauce

Salt Spring's Balsamic Chicken with Mushrooms and Sundried Cherries

Poplar Grove's Seared Duck in Cherry Merlot Reduction

Roasted Cornish Game Hens

Domaine de Chaberton's Coq au Vin

Florentine Chicken

Featuring BC White Wine

When a dish has "Florentine" in the name it usually means that it contains spinach. This is all because of Catherine Medici (1519-1589) who was born in Florence, Italy, and later married Henri II to become Queen of France. She was obsessed with spinach and insisted that it was a part of every meal. The French then dubbed dishes cooked with spinach "Florentine" after the origins of their queen.

Serves 4

INGREDIENTS

1½ cups **BC White Wine**

4 skinless, boneless chicken breasts

¼ cup flour

6 tbsp butter

¼ cup onion, finely chopped

3 garlic cloves, chopped

1 cup whipping cream

1 tbsp fresh flat leaf parsley, chopped

2 pkgs frozen spinach (10 oz each), thawed and drained

½ tsp dried basil

½ tsp dried thyme

salt and pepper to taste

1. Season the chicken with salt and pepper. Dust the chicken with the flour giving it a light coat all over. Shake off any excess.

2. Melt 2 tbsp of butter in a large frying pan over medium heat. Add the chicken, cooking for 5 minutes on each side, until brown. Remove chicken and set aside, but keep warm.

3. Melt 2 more tbsp of butter in the pan. Add the onion and 2 cloves of garlic and sauté for 3-4 minutes. Increase the heat to medium-high and add the **BC White Wine**. Stir, scraping up any bits from the bottom of the pan. Let the liquid reduce by about half then reduce the heat to a high simmer.

4. Add the cream and stir continuously. Let the mixture reduce by half again. Add the parsley and return the chicken to the pan. Make sure that the chicken is coated in the sauce and that it is cooked through before removing the pan from the heat. This should take between 5-10 minutes.

5. Meanwhile, melt the remaining butter in a separate pan over medium heat. Add the remaining garlic and sauté for 30 seconds. Add spinach, thyme and basil and season with salt and pepper to taste. Sauté until spinach is heated throughout and then transfer spinach to a serving platter.

6. Place the chicken on top of the spinach. Pour the sauce over top and serve.

Opposite: Salt Spring's Balsamic Chicken with Mushrooms and Sundried Cherries (Pg 101)
Photo: Gary Faessler

Pinot Noir Chicken with Grapes

Featuring BC Pinot Noir

Sweet, plump grapes, thyme, cream, mushrooms and chicken – does it get any better? Of course it does, by adding the Pinot Noir. This is a dish that does not require too much work to prepare and the unusual combination of grapes and chicken is sure to impress dinner guests.

Serves 4

INGREDIENTS

1 cup **BC Pinot Noir**

4 skinless, boneless chicken breasts
(6-8 oz)

1 tbsp olive oil

3 tbsp butter

1½ cups mushrooms, sliced

1 cup whipping cream

2 tbsp fresh thyme, chopped

1 small bunch seedless red grapes

salt and pepper to taste

1. Coat chicken breasts with oil and season with salt and pepper.

2. Melt butter in a sauté pan over medium heat. Add chicken breasts and cook for 5 minutes on each side, sealing in the flavour. Add mushrooms to the pan and sauté until soft and golden. Add **BC Pinot Noir** to the pan and simmer for an additional 5 minutes, allowing the wine to reduce a little.

3. Stir through cream and thyme, reduce heat and cover for 10 minutes, stirring occasionally. Remove the cover and stir, reducing until consistency is thick and creamy, then add the grapes and allow them to warm before serving.

4. This dish is delicious served on a bed of fresh pasta or wild rice, accompanied by a glass of **BC Pinot Noir**.

Opposite: The pyramid and giant wine bottle at Summerhill Pyramid Winery
Photo: Tibor "Tibby" Erdelyi

Free-Range Turkey in White Wine

Featuring BC White Wine

This recipe is an old classic enjoyed at many family Thanksgiving feasts. If Benjamin Franklin had his way the turkey would have become the national bird of the United States of America. He was dismayed when the bald eagle was chosen instead and is quoted as saying, "The turkey is a much more respectable bird." British Columbia has a wealth of free-range bird farms and we have found that the meat from free-range birds is unbeatable.

Serves 10

INGREDIENTS

1½ cups **BC White Wine**

1 free-range turkey (12 lb)

2 tsp salt

1 tsp pepper

1 tsp dried thyme

1 tsp dried rosemary

½ cup butter

1½ cups celery, chopped

1 large onion, chopped

3 whole cloves

3 tbsp flour

2 chicken or beef stock cubes

water

1. Preheat oven to 400°F. Remove the giblets and neck from the turkey. Wash the neck and set it aside. Wash the whole turkey and pat dry. In a small bowl combine salt, pepper, rosemary and thyme. Take half of this mixture and rub it inside the turkey.

2. Tie the legs together and lay the turkey in a baking pan with the breast facing up. Rub the turkey with half of the butter and sprinkle with salt and pepper.

3. Insert a meat thermometer into the thickest part of the thigh. Place the turkey in the oven for 40 minutes, checking every 10 minutes and brushing with remaining butter.

4. Reduce the temperature to 350°F. Add celery, onions, cloves and the turkey neck to the roasting pan. Pour 1 cup of **BC White Wine** over the turkey. Cover the pan entirely with aluminium foil. Roast for 2 hours, checking every 20 minutes and basting with the turkey juices.

5. Remove the foil and bake an additional 30-40 minutes or until meat thermometer reaches 185°F. Remove the turkey from the pan, remove ties and pins and let the turkey stand for 20 minutes before carving. Discard the neck.

6. Meanwhile, transfer turkey juices to a saucepan and bring to a boil over medium heat, stirring well. Simmer for 5 minutes. Strain the liquid and skim off the fat. Add enough water to make 3 cups of liquid. In a separate bowl combine remaining **BC White Wine** and flour, mixing well. Add this mixture slowly to the pan, stirring well then add the stock cubes and mix well. Simmer for additional 7 minutes before straining again. Pour into a gravy boat and place on the table.

7. Enjoy your turkey with gravy and all the trimmings.

Ortega

"To be surprised, to wonder, is to begin to understand." These words of wisdom come from the famous 20TH century Spanish philosopher, Jose Ortega y Gasset. He did not invent the grape but whoever did must have been a fan. The Ortega grape was actually created in Bavaria by crossing the Müller-Turgau and Siegerrebe varieties. The grape was only registered in 1971.

In Germany, the grape is primarily used to blend, usually with Riesling. However, here in British Columbia the conditions are wonderful for turning the Ortega grape into a rich, flowery, even peachy wine in its own right.

Ideally suited to British Columbia, the grape is very hardy and it ripens early. One of the biggest problems is that fungal diseases easily affect it and this sometimes leads to lost crops – every winemaker's nightmare.

Many wine lovers have put forward the case that the best Ortega in the world comes from the wineries on Vancouver Island. The grape has been growing there since the early 1980s. However, with so much of this wonderful wine being produced throughout the province, it is difficult to say who has achieved the best results.

This wine is superb served with salmon, seafood and rich white meats. Even Cajun and curry dishes seem to go well with this versatile wine. If you are not familiar with British Columbia's Ortega wine, we strongly recommend trying one; you will be in for a treat.

Stuffed Chicken Breast with White Wine Sauce

Featuring BC White Wine

Tender, juicy chicken stuffed with spinach and cheese, and then topped with a scrumptious white wine sauce. This is gourmet cooking made simple – a restaurant-style dish that can easily be prepared at home.

Serves 4

INGREDIENTS

1 cup **BC White Wine**

1 cup frozen spinach, thawed and drained

1 cup ricotta cheese

½ cup Swiss cheese, grated

1 egg

2 tbsp olive oil

4 large skinless, boneless chicken breast halves

1 cup chicken stock

1 tbsp Dijon mustard

1 tsp lemon juice

salt and pepper to taste

1. In a medium bowl combine spinach, ricotta, Swiss cheese, egg, salt and pepper. Set aside.

2. Place 1 chicken breast half between two layers of plastic wrap or wax paper, boned side up. Starting in the centre of the breast, gently pound the chicken with a rolling pin or the flat side of meat hammer until breasts are around ¼ inch thick. Repeat with the remaining chicken breast halves.

3. Season the meat with salt and pepper. Divide the spinach mixture in 4, placing a pile in the centre of each flattened breast. Wrap the breast around the spinach mixture like a parcel and use toothpicks to secure.

4. Heat the oil in a large pan over medium heat. Add the chicken parcels and fry for approximately 3 minutes on each side. Reduce the heat to low, cover the pan and cook for a further 6-7 minutes or until meat is cooked through. Do not overcook or the meat will dry out. Remove chicken and let it stand for 5-6 minutes.

5. Heat **BC White Wine** and stock in a saucepan over high heat, stirring frequently. Once it boils, reduce heat and simmer, reducing mixture by about one-third. Add mustard and lemon juice and stir through.

6. Cut chicken parcels into thick slices and top with the sauce. Serve immediately with your favourite vegetables or salad.

Salt Spring's Balsamic Chicken with Mushrooms and Sundried Cherries

Featuring Salt Spring Vineyards Pinot Noir

Salt Spring Pinot Noir is a dark ruby, medium-bodied Pinot with bright and juicy ripe cherry flavours and a hint of pepper and spice from barrel aging. It contains firm tannins that will continue to develop wonderfully - a gem of a wine from Salt Spring Vineyards. Colleen Bowen has created this wonderful recipe, which she prepared for the winery crew at the Salt Spring Island 2005 kick-off dinner. Another option for this recipe is to use chicken pieces on the bone.

Serves 8

INGREDIENTS

2 cups **Salt Spring Vineyards Pinot Noir**

8 boneless, skinless chicken thighs

4 tbsp flour

½ lb pancetta bacon

1 tbsp olive oil

2 onions, chopped

8 garlic cloves, finely chopped

½ cup mushrooms, sliced

1 cup dried cherries, chopped (available in health food stores)

½ cup good quality balsamic vinegar

½ cup chicken stock

salt and pepper

1. Dredge chicken in flour seasoned with salt and pepper.

2. Over medium-high heat fry pancetta in olive oil until crisp. Remove from the pan and set aside. Brown chicken on both sides in bacon fat then remove from the pan. Sauté onion, garlic and mushrooms until soft.

3. Add cherries, **Salt Spring Vineyards Pinot Noir**, vinegar, chicken stock, pancetta and chicken and simmer over medium-low heat for 30 minutes. Check the seasoning and adjust with balsamic vinegar if necessary.

4. Serve with green beans and mashed potatoes and of course a glass of **Salt Spring Vineyards Pinot Noir**.

Salt Spring Vineyards

Location: 151 Lee Road, Salt Spring Island, BC

Telephone/Fax: (250) 653-9463 / (250) 653-9464

Website and Email: www.saltspringvineyards.com, vineyards@saltspring.com

Wine Shop, Tours and Tastings: Tastings May-Sep, daily noon-5pm; Feb, Mar, Apr, Oct, Dec, Sat noon-5pm.

Getting There: At the top of the big hill, 6km from the Fulford ferry terminal. At the corner of the 1700 block of Fulford-Ganges Road and Lee Road.

Highlights: Try the estate Pinot Noir, Pinot Gris, Chardonnay, Millotage and the organic Blackberry Port. (Who would encourage blackberries to grow?)

Merlot

PRONOUNCED (MARE-LOW)

HISTORIANS HAVE TRACED MERLOT AS FAR BACK AS FIRST CENTURY FRANCE. MERLOT IS ONE OF THE ACCLAIMED RED VARIETIES OF BORDEAUX, WHERE IT BECAME FAMOUS DURING IN THE 1800S. THIS WINE IS A LITTLE SOFTER AND PERHAPS WARMER THAN CABERNET SAUVIGNON.

THE WINE HAS BEEN GROWING IN POPULARITY SINCE THE LATE 1970S WHEN WINEMAKERS IN NORTH AMERICA DISCOVERED THAT THE GRAPE IS NOT ONLY GOOD FOR BLENDING, BUT THAT IT ALSO PRODUCES WONDERFUL WINE ON ITS OWN. IT IS GENERALLY BELIEVED THAT THE OLDEST MERLOT VINES IN THE PROVINCE ARE FOUND AT CEDAR CREEK VINEYARD. THESE WERE PLANTED SOMETIME DURING THE 1970S.

MERLOT GRAPES MATURE EARLIER AND ARE LARGER THAN THE CABERNET SAUVIGNON GRAPE. THEY ALSO HAVE A THICKER SKIN. THIS WINE IS NOT GREAT FOR LONG-TERM CELLARING, UNLESS IT IS BLENDED. THIS PROBABLY ACCOUNTS FOR SOME OF ITS RECENT POPULARITY, AS MANY CONSUMERS PREFER THE CONVENIENCE OF HAVING A GREAT WINE TO DRINK IMMEDIATELY RATHER THAN WAITING FOR THE CELLARING PROCESS.

COMMON CHARACTERISTICS DISPLAYED IN MERLOT WINES INCLUDE, PLUM, BLACKCURRANT, CHERRY, VANILLA AND CLOVES. THE WINE PAIRS WELL WITH LAMB, GRILLED MEATS, WILD GAME, HEARTY PASTAS, DUCK AND AGED CHEESES.

Poplar Grove's Seared Duck in Cherry Merlot Reduction

Featuring Poplar Grove Benchmark Merlot

Our Merlot shows complex blackberry and cherry on a background of toasty French oak. The clean acid, robust ripe tannins and long finish make it good food wine, pairing well with large flavours and rich, creamy textures. A great way to begin this recipe is to pour a large glass of Merlot for the chef and a smaller glass for any onlookers!

Serves 6

INGREDIENTS

1 cup **Poplar Grove Benchmark Merlot**

6 duck pieces (leg, breast, etc.)

3 tbsp black peppercorns, crushed

kosher salt

3 tbsp corn oil

3 tbsp shallots, minced

¾ cup strong chicken stock

$^1/_3$ cup sundried Okanagan cherries, soaked in hot water until plump

9 sprigs of parsley, chopped

6 tbsp unsalted butter

salt and pepper to taste

1. Fill up the chef's glass. Pat the duck dry if necessary, coat each side evenly with a good amount of pepper and salt and rub in. Set the skillet over high heat and film the pan with oil. When oil is just beginning to smoke add 2 or 3 pieces of duck and sear each side for 2-3 minutes or until brown and crusty. Remove from the pan. Reheat the pan to sear off the remaining pieces of duck. Keep seared duck in a warm place.

2. Top up the chef's glass. Pour off the excess oil from the pan and place it back on the heat. Add the shallots and sauté until they are soft. Add the **Poplar Grove Benchmark Merlot**, chicken stock, drained soaked cherries and parsley and boil until reduced by half. Add the butter and any juices that have extruded from the duck. Let it boil to thicken and blend the flavours.

3. Return duck to the pan and simmer to finish for about 5 minutes or until cooked through to medium. Arrange duck pieces on a plate and spoon the sauce over them. Open another bottle of **Poplar Grove Benchmark Merlot** and enjoy.

Poplar Grove Winery

Location: 1060 Poplar Grove Road, Penticton, BC

Telephone: (250) 492-4575

Website: www.poplargrove.ca, wine@poplargrove.ca

Wine Shop, Tours and Tastings: Wine shop will be open during the summer 11am-5pm.

Getting There: A short drive along Naramata Bench towards the Naramata village. Turn down Poplar Grove Road towards the lake and it becomes the driveway.

Highlights: Poplar Grove is also the home of Poplar Grove Artisan Cheese. They make Double Cream Camembert, Naramata Blue and Harvest Moon Washed Rind.

Roasted Cornish Game Hens

Featuring BC White Wine

When you buy Cornish game hens you might actually be buying roosters! Both the male and female of the species are sold under the same name. Luckily both genders are equally tasty. These birds are excellent for roasting and they are very simple to cook. It is normal to allow one hen per person, but if you have exceptionally large hens, you might want to consider reducing this to a half bird.

Serves 6

INGREDIENTS

½ cup **BC White Wine**

6 Cornish game hens

2 lemons, quartered

1 medium onion, cut into 6 wedges

3 sprigs of basil, halved

6 tbsp butter

salt and pepper

1. Preheat the oven to 350°F. Rinse the game hens and pat them dry. Season the cavity with salt and pepper. Place a wedge of lemon, a wedge of onion and half a sprig of basil inside the cavity of each bird. Rub the remaining lemon wedges over the outside of each bird squeezing out a little juice onto each.

2. Dot the butter over the birds, using 1 tbsp for each bird. Then pour the **BC White Wine** into the roasting pan and place the tray into the oven.

3. Bake for 45 minutes to 1 hour. When you pierce the thickest part of the thigh and the juices run clear, you will know that the bird is done. Remove the birds from the oven and cover with foil, letting them stand for 10 minutes to redistribute the juices throughout the flesh before serving. Serve with the juices from the pan spooned over the top.

Domaine de Chaberton's Coq au Vin

Featuring Chaberton Rouge

Chaberton Rouge is a blend of Merlot, Gamay Noir and Cabernet Sauvignon, making it a complement to any flavourful dish. It is light to medium in body with soft, fresh berry notes and a touch of spice on the finish. This wine won gold at the 2004 All Canadian Wine Championship in Ontario.

Serves 4-6

INGREDIENTS

2 bottles **Chaberton Rouge**	2 tbsp vegetable oil
1 cup each of onion, celery, carrots, diced	3½ oz bacon, diced
1 bouquet garni (See pg 63)	1 cup shallots, diced
1 whole roaster chicken, cut into 8 pieces	3 cups mushrooms, cut in wedges
	3½ oz dark chocolate, chopped
	salt and pepper
1 cup flour	1 bunch parsley, chopped for garnish

1. Combine **Chaberton Rouge**, onion, celery, carrots and bouquet garni in a large container. Add chicken, cover and marinate overnight in wine mixture.

2. Remove chicken from marinade and reserve the mixture. Preheat oven to 325°F. Season chicken with salt and pepper, and coat in flour. In a large ovenproof skillet, heat oil and sear chicken until golden brown. Add marinade and bring to a boil. Cover and place in oven for 1-2 hours, until chicken is tender.

3. While chicken is cooking, fry bacon and shallots in a separate pan then add mushrooms and stir well until cooked. Remove and set side. Remove cooked chicken pieces from oven and keep warm. Transfer cooking juice to saucepan and reduce to a sauce consistency. Season if necessary, add chocolate, stir thoroughly and remove from heat.

4. Cover chicken with sauce and serve with the mushrooms and bacon. Garnish with parsley and enjoy with a glass of **Chaberton Rouge**.

Domaine de Chaberton

Location: 1064-216th Street Langley, BC

Telephone/Fax: (604) 530-1736/ (604) 533-9687

Bistro Reservations: (604) 530-9694

Website and Email: www.domainedechaberton.com, info@domainedechaberton.com

Wine Shop, Tours and Tastings: Open Mon-Sat, 10am-6pm; Sun 11am-6pm. Public tours at 2pm & 4pm (weather permitting). Tastings anytime.

Getting There: From Vancouver head east on Highway 1. Take the 200 Street South exit. Turn left at the intersection of 16th Avenue and then right on 216th Street. Watch for the "Wine Route" sign.

Highlights: Award-winning wines, gift baskets and wine accessories. Home of the famous Bacchus Bistro for authentic French cuisine.

Meat

During one of my treks through Afghanistan, we lost our corkscrew.
We were compelled to live on food and water for several days.

Cuthbert J. Twillie (W.C. Fields) in My Little Chickadee, *1940*

La Frenz Roasted Leg of Lamb

Chalet Estate's Bistro Braised Beef

Succulent Gamay Souvlaki

Merlot Buffalo Steaks

Garlic Roast Pork

Laughing Stock's Filet Mignon au Portfolio

River's Bend Braised Lamb Shank with Gremolata

Beef Stroganoff

St. Hubertus Zurich Geschnetzeltes

Braised Beef Short Ribs

Rouladen

Chardonnay Pork Chops

Gourmet Sloppy Joes "Nichol Style"

Pemberton Valley Elk Loin Medallions with Blueberry and Tantalus Sauce

Herder's Venison Steaks with Cranberry

La Frenz Roasted Leg of Lamb

Featuring La Frenz Shiraz

La Frenz Shiraz made its debut in 2004 with the 2002 vintage. Harvested from our vineyards on the Naramata Bench it quickly became known as an "Aussie" style benchmark Shiraz. Super ripe fruit created a powerful, full-bodied, richly coloured and flavoured Shiraz – opulent and silky with flavours of violet, plums and blueberries. The best quality new French oak was used to bolster, rather than mask, the concentrated fruit of this wine.

Serves 4

INGREDIENTS

¼ cup **La Frenz Shiraz**

1 leg of lamb

3 garlic cloves, halved

1 tbsp butter

1 tbsp olive oil

2 tbsp instant coffee powder (or ½ cup strong coffee)

2 shallots, chopped

2 tbsp mustard

½ cup chicken stock

1 tbsp flour

1-2 tbsp red currant jelly

½ cup cream

salt and pepper

1. Preheat oven to 350°F. Trim excess fat from the lamb and pat dry with paper towel. Season well with salt and pepper. Stab the leg to the bone 6 times and insert halved garlic cloves in each cut. In a large skillet over medium heat brown leg well on all sides in butter and olive oil, before transferring the leg to an ovenproof dish, preferably a Dutch oven.

2. In a separate bowl mix coffee, shallots, mustard, chicken stock and **La Frenz Shiraz** and pour mixture over lamb. Cover and transfer to oven. Roast 45 minutes for rare or 1 hour for well-done. Baste or turn over leg twice during cooking. When cooked, remove leg and place on a carving board.

3. Reduce pan juices on stovetop to half, then add flour and mix well to form a roux. When thoroughly mixed, add 1-2 tbsp red current jelly and continue mixing. Add cream and stir while simmering, until gravy thickens.

4. Carve lamb into slices and serve with gravy. This meal is delicious with potatoes, ratatouille and a glass of **La Frenz Shiraz**.

La Frenz Winery

Location: 740 Naramata Road, Penticton, BC

Telephone/Fax: (250) 492-6690 / (250) 492-6916

Website and Email: www.lafrenzwinery.com, lafrenz@shaw.ca

Wine Shop, Tours and Tastings: Open for tastings and sales May - mid-Oct, 10am-5pm. By appointment for the rest of the year, for sales only. Tours by appointment.

Getting There: Take Highway 97 to Penticton. Follow signs to Naramata Bench wineries. On Naramata Road look for the LA FRENZ sign. Turn up Randolf Road. Only 5 minutes from Penticton city centre.

Highlights: La Frenz is recognised as one of BC's premier boutique wine producers. Wines are crafted by Australian winemaker Jeff Martin. Voted "winery to watch" in 2004. Spectacular views as seen on the 1954 $100 bill.

Chalet Estate's Bistro Braised Beef

Featuring Chalet Estate Gamay Noir

Chalet Estate Vineyard Gamay Noir is a fruit forward, medium weight wine with hints of black cherry and vanilla. This wine pairs magnificently with red meats and tomato dishes.

Serves 12

INGREDIENTS

1 cup **Chalet Estate Gamay Noir**	1 tbsp Dijon mustard
2 blade pot roasts (3 lbs each)	1 tsp dried thyme
¼ cup plain flour	1 tsp dried rosemary
¼ cup vegetable oil	2 bay leaves
2 large onions, chopped	1-3 tbsp cornstarch
4 large carrots, thickly sliced	salt and pepper
1 can undiluted beef broth (10 oz)	

1. Preheat oven to 350°F. Slice each roast in half. Combine flour, salt and pepper in a plastic bag. One at a time, place each piece of meat in the bag and coat. Set meat aside and save flour for later. Heat 2 tbsp oil over medium-high heat in a large ovenproof saucepan and brown each piece of meat for 3 minutes on each side. Add more oil if needed. Set browned meat aside on a plate.

2. Reduce heat to medium and add onions and carrots, sprinkling leftover flour over top. Stir for 3 minutes. Gradually stir in broth and using a wooden spoon, scrape up bits from the bottom of the pan. Stir in **Chalet Estate Gamay Noir**, mustard, thyme, rosemary and bay leaves. Bring to a boil then submerge the meat in the liquid. Cover and place in oven for 3 hours or until meat is fork tender. Turn meat halfway through cooking. When done, remove meat and cover with foil, allow meat to stand for 10 minutes before slicing.

3. Skim the fat from the top of the vegetables and discard. Transfer sauce to a large measuring cup. For every cup of sauce, mix 1 tbsp cornstarch with 2 tbsp water in a small bowl and stir until smooth. Return sauce and vegetables to the pan, add cornstarch mix to sauce and bring to a boil. Stir until thickened. Slice meat and then serve topped with sauce and vegetables. Serve with a glass of **Chalet Estate Gamay Noir**.

Chalet Estate Vineyard

Location: 11195 Chalet Road, North Saanich, BC

Telephone/Fax: (250) 656-2552 / (250) 656-9719

Website and Email: www.chaletestatevineyard.ca, chaletestate@shaw.ca

Wine Shop, Tours and Tastings: Wine shop open Tue-Sun 11am-5pm. Tastings, wine patio and gift shop.

Getting There: On the Pat Bay Highway take the Wain Road exit and follow the signs. Across from Deep Cove Chalet Restaurant.

Highlights: A small boutique winery. The home of award-winning Ortega wine.

Gamay Noir

PRONOUNCED (GA-MAY NA-WHAR)

IT WAS 1395 WHEN PHILLIP THE BOLD, DUKE OF NORMANDY, ORDERED ALL OF THE GAMAY NOIR VINES TO BE RIPPED OUT OF THE GROUND IN BURGUNDY. HE EVEN INTRODUCED A LAW SAYING THAT THE VARIETY WOULD NEVER BE ALLOWED TO GROW IN BURGUNDY AGAIN. HIS REASONING WAS THAT PINOT NOIR WOULD BE BROUGHT IN TO REPLACE THE OUTGOING VINES.

FORTUNATELY THE GRAPE FOUND A NEW HOME IN NEARBY BEAUJOLAIS. FROM THERE IT HAS EVENTUALLY MADE ITS WAY TO BRITISH COLUMBIA, WHERE IT IS DELIGHTING THE PALATES OF WINE LOVERS TODAY. THE NAME IS SOMETIMES SHORTENED TO GAMAY.

THE GAMAY NOIR GRAPE IS ONE OF THE FIRST TO BUD AND FLOWER, WHICH MAKES IT A POTENTIAL VICTIM FOR SPRING FROSTS. IT USUALLY RIPENS AROUND HALFWAY THROUGH THE SEASON. LIKE THE WINES IN BEAUJOLAIS, GAMAY NOIR DOES NOT TAKE LONG TO GO FROM THE VINE TO THE STORE, WHICH IS A GREAT ADVANTAGE FOR GROWERS. THIS IS NOT RECOGNISED AS A WINE TO CELLAR AND MOST FEEL THAT IT IS BEST WHEN YOUNG.

GAMAY NOIR IS GENERALLY A LIGHT COLOURED RED WINE THAT IS OFTEN VERY FRAGRANT. THE WINES CAN BE TANGY AND FULL OF FRUIT. GAMAY NOIR CAN BE SERVED SLIGHTLY CHILLED AND IT MAKES A GREAT ACCOMPANIMENT TO RED MEATS, TOMATO DISHES, BARBEQUED FOOD OR CHEESE AND CRACKERS.

Succulent Gamay Souvlaki

Featuring BC Gamay Noir

Souvlakis are to the Greeks what hamburgers are to North Americans. They are a popular meal or snack that have become a recognised part of the culture. Of course souvlaki is much healthier! We have used Gamay Noir in this recipe but you can substitute that for your favourite BC Red Wine if you like.

Serves 4-8

INGREDIENTS

¾ cup **BC Gamay Noir**	2 tsp salt
1½ lbs lamb, cut in 1 inch cubes	4-8 pita breads
½ cup olive oil	2 tomatoes, sliced
3 garlic cloves, crushed	1 red onion, sliced
1 tsp dried oregano	½ cucumber, sliced
1 tbsp dried mint	1 cup tzatziki dressing

1. In a sealed container combine lamb, oil, **BC Gamay Noir**, garlic, mint, oregano and salt. Make sure lamb is well coated and then refrigerate for at least 5 hours, preferably overnight.

2. Preheat the grill and brush the grate with olive oil. Thread lamb cubes onto metal skewers or wooden skewers that have been pre-soaked in water for about 30 minutes (to avoid burning). Place on the grill for about 10 minutes, turning frequently. When meat is cooked, remove.

3. Place the pitas on the grill for a minute to heat them. Serve lamb on the pitas with onion, tomato and cucumber, topped with tzatziki.

4. This meal is wonderful served with a rice pilaf and is best accompanied by a glass of **BC Gamay Noir.**

Chef's Easy Tzatziki Recipe

Using the back of a spoon, mash a large clove of crushed garlic into a generous pinch of salt and mash into a paste. Add 2 cups of Greek style plain yoghurt to the garlic. Grate a cucumber and squeeze to extract as much juice as possible, discarding the juice. Add the cucumber to the yoghurt with a dash of lemon juice. Stir well to thoroughly combine, cover and allow the mix to sit refrigerated for at least 1 hour so that the flavour becomes infused. Serve as a sauce on the souvlaki or separately as a dip with pita.

Merlot Buffalo Steaks

Featuring BC Merlot

Buffalo meat has a much lower fat content than beef. This means that if you overcook the meat it will become dry. The best way to experience the quality of the meat is to eat the steaks either rare or medium rare. Keep an eye on the steaks as buffalo cooks faster than beef. If you have never eaten buffalo it tends to be richer and fuller tasting than beef and it is not at all "gamey".

Serves 4

INGREDIENTS

1½ cups **BC Merlot**

4 tbsp butter

1½ tbsp olive oil

4 BC buffalo steaks (6-8 oz)

¼ cup shallots, chopped

2 tbsp fresh tarragon, chopped

3 tbsp whipping cream

1. Heat 2 tbsp butter with oil in a sauté pan over medium heat. Add the steaks when oil is hot. Brown steaks for 4-5 minutes on each side (medium rare) or until they reach desired "doneness". Remove steaks from pan and set aside. Keep warm.

2. Add shallots and tarragon to the pan and sauté for 2-3 minutes. Add **BC Merlot** and stir with a wooden spoon, scraping up any bits from the bottom of the pan. Reduce to about $^{1}/_{3}$ of a cup, then add cream and continue stirring for 2-3 minutes but do not let the sauce boil.

3. Remove from the heat and stir through the remaining butter. Serve the steaks topped with the Merlot cream sauce accompanied by new potatoes and your favourite vegetables.

Opposite: River's Bend Braised Lamb Shanks with Gremolata (Pg 116)
Photo: Gary Faessler with food prepared by John Waller

Garlic Roast Pork

Featuring BC Pinot Noir

This variation of a classic Cuban recipe is a favourite of garlic lovers!

Serves 8

INGREDIENTS

1 cup **BC Pinot Noir**	1 tsp dried oregano
5 garlic cloves, crushed	1 boneless pork roast (5-6 lbs)
1 tsp dried rosemary	6 garlic cloves, halved

1. In a small bowl, mix together crushed garlic, rosemary, oregano and **BC Pinot Noir**. Place roast in a large plastic or glass container, add marinade and cover. Marinate overnight.

2. Preheat oven to 325°F. Transfer pork roast to a Dutch oven. Make 12 1-inch slits in the meat with a sharp knife and insert a garlic half in each slit. Pour marinade over the meat and cover.

3. Roast for 35 minutes per pound or until a meat thermometer inserted into the centre of the roast reads at least 160°F.

4. Let sit for 10 minutes before slicing and serve with your favourite vegetables and a glass of **BC Pinot Noir**.

Opposite: LaRose Vineyard, Osoyoos, BC
Photo: Brian Sprout courtesy of Vincor

Laughing Stock's Filet Mignon au Portfolio

Featuring Laughing Stock Portfolio

Just like assembling a stock portfolio, putting together a blended wine takes finesse and judgement so that the sum will be greater than the individual parts. We believe that our inaugural release captures our goal of creating a world-class "Bordeaux" by combining first-class grapes and highly reputable winemaking. Portfolio 2003 is composed of Merlot 64%, Cabernet Sauvignon 33% and Cabernet Franc 3%. It is aged for 18 months in barrel and 6 months in bottle, with 500 cases produced.

Serves 4

INGREDIENTS

4 filet mignon steaks (7 oz)

1 tbsp canola or olive oil

salt and pepper

sprigs of fresh parsley and thyme for garnish

1. Preheat a heavy skillet or grill until very hot, so that when cooking the meat the outside will be seared, caramelising the meat's natural sugars and juices.

2. Lightly season the filet with salt and pepper and lightly brush the meat with oil. Cook to taste. Cooking time depends on the thickness of the meat and preference.

3. Place the filets on warm serving plates and ladle warm portfolio sauce over the meat. Garnish with the fresh thyme and parsley sprigs and serve immediately. Serve with a glass of **Laughing Stock Portfolio**.

Laughing Stock Vineyards

Location: 1548 Naramata Road, Penticton, BC

Telephone / Fax: (250) 493-8466 / (250) 492-2363

Website and Email: www.laughingstock.ca, info@laughingstock.ca

Wine Shop, Tours and Tastings: The tasting room will open in Fall 2005, in time for the wine festival. Please call ahead to confirm hours.

Getting There: Located on Naramata Bench, which is on the east side of Okanagan Lake, just north of Penticton.

Highlights: Located on the picturesque Naramata Bench, Laughing Stock Vineyards is a serious enterprise with a light-hearted attitude. With a name like Laughing Stock, they wake up everyday with the motivation not to live up to their name. Thus they aim to produce the highest quality small production wines from the burgeoning Okanagan Valley. What choice do they have?

Portfolio Sauce

INGREDIENTS

1¼ cups **Laughing Stock Portfolio**

7 tbsp butter

2 Portabella mushrooms, halved then cut in ¼ inch x 1 inch strips

1 garlic clove, crushed

½ cup shallots, finely chopped

1 sprig of fresh thyme

1 sprig of fresh parsley

1 small bay leaf

1 tbsp white peppercorns, crushed

1 cup veal stock (available from a good butcher)

1 tsp fresh thyme leaves

1 tsp fresh parsley, chopped

salt and pepper to taste

1. Over medium heat, melt half of the butter and sauté the mushrooms until brown. Add garlic and shallots and cook for 4-5 minutes, stirring occasionally.

2. After the shallots and garlic have lightly browned, deglaze the pan with a few tbsp of **Laughing Stock Portfolio**.

3. Add the remaining **Laughing Stock Portfolio**, sprigs of thyme and parsley, bay leaf and crushed peppercorns and bring to a boil. Stir frequently to ensure mushrooms and shallots don't stick to the bottom of the pan and burn.

4. Boil until the liquid is reduced by a third and then add the veal stock. Cook over low heat for 20 minutes.

5. Discard the parsley, thyme and bay leaf. Using a whisk beat in the remaining butter. Add the fresh thyme leaves and chopped parsley. Season with salt and pepper. Remove from the heat, but keep warm.

River's Bend Braised Lamb Shank with Gremolata

Featuring River's Bend Merlot

Gary Faessler, renowned food and wine expert, created this superb autumn dish. The lamb becomes meltingly soft, juicy and fall-off-the-bone tender after cooking in aromatic braising liquids. The gremolata is a traditional garnish made from chopped parsley, minced garlic and lemon zest that imparts a fresh citrus note to compliment this rich and meaty dish. The 2001 Merlot is aged in French oak and is blended with a small addition of Cabernet Franc and Sauvignon, producing an elegant wine with friendly tannins. The Merlot is deep garnet in colour with flavours of black cherry, black currant, dark plum, chocolate and spice.

Serves 4

INGREDIENTS

2 cups **River's Bend Merlot**

3 tbsp flat leaf parsley, chopped

1 tsp lemon zest, minced

1 large garlic clove, minced

3 tbsp extra virgin olive oil

4 lamb shanks

½ cup flour

1 medium onion, finely diced

1 carrot, finely diced

1 rib of celery, finely diced

4 garlic cloves, chopped

3 bay leaves

2 tbsp each of fresh thyme, oregano and sage, chopped

1 can diced tomatoes (12 oz)

2 cups lamb or beef stock

salt and pepper

1. Make the gremolata by mixing together the parsley, lemon zest and minced garlic clove.

2. Preheat the oven to 325°F. Add the olive oil to a large casserole dish over medium-high heat. Season the lamb shanks with salt and pepper. Dredge the shanks in the flour, coating each side completely. When oil is hot, sear the shanks until very brown on all sides, about 3 minutes each side. Don't crowd the pan – brown two shanks at a time if pan does not accommodate all four.

3. Remove the shanks and set aside. Reduce the heat to medium. Add the onion, celery and carrots to the pot and sauté for 3 minutes. Stir in the chopped garlic, bay leaves, thyme, oregano and sage. Cook for 1 minute. Deglaze the pan with the **River's Bend Merlot**, scraping the bottom and sides to loosen the browned particles. Add the stock and tomatoes. Bring the liquid to a boil then reduce immediately to a simmer. Place the shanks back in the pan, making sure they are submerged at least halfway.

4. Cover the casserole and braise shanks in the middle of the oven, basting occasionally, until the sauce is stew-like and the meat is very tender, about 2 hours. Remove the bay leaves, sprinkle gremolata over the lamb shanks and serve over mashed potatoes or polenta with a glass of **River's Bend Merlot.**

Court Faessler at River's Bend Vineyard. Photo: Linda Faessler.

A NOTE FROM RIVER'S BEND WINERY

Opened in the spring of 2005, River's Bend is a boutique winery located on 28 acres of pastoral farmland alongside the winding banks of the Serpentine River in South Surrey, British Columbia. First planted in 1990, in a gem of a microclimate, the winery's 14-acre vineyard yields numerous grape varieties including Pinot Noir, Gamay, Gewürztraminer, Pinot Gris and Chardonnay. The grapes are grown using natural farming methods; the wines, gently handcrafted and bottled at their peak to preserve their delicate aroma and flavour. A further six acres of land is available for future planting.

Owner Court Faessler (shown above; Faessler is Swiss for wine barrel maker) is producing some lovely wines, including an elegant non-oaked Chardonnay, beautifully balanced with clean tropical, green apple and citrus flavours, followed by a long, lingering honey and lemon finish. The Pinot Gris has a spicy and floral aroma with discreet pear, cantaloupe and pink grapefruit notes. The luscious Pinot Noir is unfiltered and lightly oaked with nice tannins. Its generous smoky finish follows strawberry, cranberry and cracked black pepper notes.

We invite you to visit the winery and tour the vineyards and wine-making facilities. In our wine store and tasting room we offer fine wines and a fireplace furnishes warmth on cooler, wet afternoons. On sunnier days, what better way to enjoy a glass of River's Bend wine than to bring a picnic and lunch 'al fresco' on the winery's expansive patio overlooking lush vineyards. Please, come join us for a taste of British Columbia at River's Bend Winery.

River's Bend Winery

Location: 15560 Colebrook Road, Surrey, BC

Telephone: (604) 574-6106

Website and Email: www.riversbendwinery.com, gfaessler@shaw.ca

Wine Shop, Tours and Tastings: Wine shop and tasting room open Tues-Sun 11am-6pm. Tours starting in early Summer 2005, daily at 3pm.

Getting There: Take Highway 1 south from Vancouver, over the Port Mann Bridge and take exit 48, keeping right on the ramp onto 152nd Street. Turn left (east) onto Colebrook Road to River's Bend Winery.

Highlights: Fully equipped wine laboratory with a friendly atmosphere. A great place for a picnic. Of course, the other highlight is the wonderful wine.

Beef Stroganoff

Featuring BC Red Wine

100 years ago, Count Pavel Alexandrovich Stroganov was a Russian celebrity. He was a good friend of Alexander III and he loved to entertain and host magnificent dinner parties. It is rumoured that this dish was served at one of those lavish affairs and it has retained the Count's name ever since. It is not known whether they actually used BC red wine in the original but I bet it would have tasted better if they did.

Serves 4

INGREDIENTS

¾ cup **BC Red Wine**

4 tbsp butter

1 lb beef tenderloin, cut into strips

1 small onion, chopped

1 cup fresh mushrooms, sliced

1 tbsp flour

½ cup beef stock

¼ cup sour cream

1 tbsp Dijon mustard

1 package of egg noodles (8 oz)

salt and pepper to taste

¼ cup fresh parsley, chopped for garnish

1. Melt 2 tbsp of butter in a large sauté pan over medium-high heat. Season meat to taste with salt and pepper and then add to the pan. Brown meat and then add onion and mushrooms. Sauté for another 5 minutes then set aside.

2. Prepare egg noodles according to directions on the package.

3. In a separate large pan, mix remaining butter with flour over medium heat until well combined. Slowly stir in the stock and the **BC Red Wine**. Bring to a boil and then add the beef and mushroom mix. Stir for 1 minute then add sour cream and mustard and mix through. Remove from the heat.

4. When egg noodles are al dente, serve on individual plates topped with beef stroganoff mixture. Garnish with chopped parsley.

Pinot Blanc

Pronounced (Pee-no-blahn)

Pinot Blanc is sometimes unfairly referred to as the poor man's Chardonnay. This is unfair because when it is done right, the wine rivals even the best Chardonnay.

Pinot Blanc is a mutation of Pinot Gris, which itself is a mutation of the Pinot Noir variety. The grape is thought to originate in the Burgundy region of France but it is now predominantly grown in the Alsace region.

In British Columbia, Pinot Blanc is also known by its Italian name "Pinot Bianco". The grape made its first appearance here during the 1970s and it has become very popular since.

The grape looks so much like Chardonnay that in some vineyards in Europe the two varieties are intermingled. Common characteristics of the wine include aromas of apple, vanilla, almonds and hazelnuts. This wine pairs well with seafood, light pastas, and pork. It also makes a great aperitif served with olives and cheese.

St. Hubertus Zurich Geschnetzeltes

Featuring St. Hubertus Pinot Blanc

Rich pear and citrus aromas on the nose with lively acid on the finish, this wine is a true example of a cool-climate wine. The palate is full and creamy, with a dry finish.

Serves 4

INGREDIENTS

½ cup **St. Hubertus Pinot Blanc**

1 lb fresh mushrooms, sliced

½ cup fresh lemon juice

1 lb veal, sliced in small, thin strips

4 tbsp vegetable oil

3 tbsp butter

1 tbsp flour

1 tbsp shallots, chopped

½ cup whipping cream

½ cup chicken stock

salt and pepper to taste

1. In a large pan, over medium heat, combine mushrooms and lemon juice. Cover and simmer for 5-10 minutes. Drain remaining liquid into a cup and set it aside.

2. Season meat with salt and pepper. Heat oil in a separate frying pan over medium-high heat. Add meat and fry until it darkens and loses all red colouring, then remove it from the pan and set aside.

3. Melt the butter in the pan and sauté shallots until soft. Add flour and stir well, absorbing the fat. Add stock and reserved liquid from the mushrooms, slowly whilst stirring continuously. Bring to a boil then add **St. Hubertus Pinot Blanc.**

4. Allow sauce to simmer before returning meat to the pan and adding mushrooms. Heat well and then add whipping cream; do not allow cream to boil. More wine and cream can be added if the sauce is too thick.

5. This delicious, hearty Swiss recipe is magnificent paired with a glass of **Oak Bay Pinot Meunier**.

St. Hubertus Estate Winery

Location: 5225 Lakeshore Road, Kelowna, BC

Telephone/Fax: (250) 764-7888 / (250) 764-0499

Website and Email: www.st-hubertus.bc.ca, wine@st-hubertus.bc.ca

Wine Shop, Tours and Tastings: Wine shop open summer, daily 10am-5:30pm; winter, Tue-Sat noon-5pm. Tastings are free.

Getting There: The winery is 11km south of downtown Kelowna on the shores of Lake Okanagan.

Highlights: The original winery was destroyed by fire in 2003. Now surrounded by wilderness, the winery is an excellent place to enjoy the views and have a picnic in the vineyard or on the beach.

Braised Beef Short Ribs

Featuring BC Red Wine

This is a wonderful dish for winter. Try curling up in front of an open fire whilst savouring this tender, succulent, braised meat as it falls off the bone. Now take a glass of BC red wine and toast your best friend or lover. This is what life is all about!

Serves 4

INGREDIENTS

1½ cups **BC Red Wine**

2 lbs beef short ribs, cut to1½ inch pieces

¼ cup vegetable oil

2 medium carrots, chopped

2 celery stalks, chopped

1 large onion, chopped

4 garlic cloves, chopped

1 bay leaf

2 sprigs thyme

3 cups beef stock

3 canned anchovy fillets

salt and pepper to taste

1. Preheat oven to 350°F. Season ribs with salt and pepper. Heat vegetable oil in a large braising dish. Add ribs and fry until all sides are browned and then remove them. Remove any fat from the pan. Add vegetables and garlic and sauté for 2-3 minutes, then add **BC Red Wine**, bay leaf and thyme. Reduce the liquid in the pan by about half and then return the ribs to the pan. Add just enough stock to cover the ribs completely, bring to a boil and then remove from heat.

2. Cover the pan and place in preheated oven. Cook for 3½ hours or until the meat is tender and falling off the bone. Remove the meat from the pan and set aside. Strain liquid into a saucepan and simmer over low heat until it is reduced by half. Add anchovies and then run the mixture through a blender or food processor until smooth.

3. Serve the ribs with the sauce. Recommended accompaniments include mashed potatoes and your favourite steamed greens along with a glass of your favourite **BC Red Wine**.

Rouladen

Featuring BC Red Wine

This family favourite is a variation of a German classic. Makes great leftovers, but we'd be surprised if there are any!

Serves 4

INGREDIENTS

½ cup **BC Red Wine**

4 very thin round steaks (6 oz)

¼ tsp salt

¼ tsp pepper

2 tsp Dijon mustard

2-3 large pickles, cut in thin strips

8 strips bacon, chopped

1 large onion, chopped

¼ cup vegetable oil

1 cup hot beef broth

5 peppercorns

1 bay leaf

1 tbsp cornstarch

3 tbsp water

1. Lay steaks on flat surface (pound with a meat mallet if they are not thin) and sprinkle with salt and pepper. Spread each steak with mustard. Divide pickles, bacon and onion evenly among steaks, then roll up like a jellyroll and secure each with a toothpick or string.

2. Heat oil in a heavy saucepan, add the steak rolls and brown well on all sides. Add hot beef broth, **BC Red Wine**, peppercorns and bay leaf. Cover and simmer for 1 hour and 20 minutes.

3. Remove steak rolls, discard toothpick or string and place on a preheated platter.

4. Blend cornstarch and water in a small bowl and add to gravy, stirring continuously. Bring to a boil, then reduce heat and simmer until thick and bubbly. Add salt and pepper, if necessary.

5. Serve Rouladen with spaetzle or egg noodles and baby carrots.

Chardonnay Pork Chops

Featuring BC Chardonnay

It is amazing how much of the wine's flavour the pork will absorb, so it is important to use a Chardonnay that you really enjoy. That should not be hard with so many wonderful BC wines to choose from.

Serves 4

INGREDIENTS

1½ cups **BC Chardonnay**

2 tbsp flour

¾ tsp dry mustard

¼ tsp salt

½ tsp black pepper

4 pork chops (8 oz)

2 tbsp butter

1 onion, chopped

1 cup cold beef stock

1. Put 1 tbsp of flour, mustard, salt and pepper in a plastic bag and mix well. Shake the chops in the bag until well-coated.

2. Melt the butter in a pan and sauté the onions over medium heat. After 2 minutes add the pork chops, browning both sides.

3. Reduce to a simmer, add ½ cup **BC Chardonnay** and cover. Simmer for 60 minutes, adding additional ¼ cup of **BC Chardonnay** every 15 minutes, or as needed to keep simmering.

4. Remove the chops, add the remaining flour and mix. Slowly add the stock, whisking well. Increase to medium heat and stir well until the gravy thickens.

5. Smother pork chops with gravy and serve over rice with fresh vegetables. Enjoy with a glass of **BC Chardonnay**.

Gourmet Sloppy Joes "Nichol Style"

Featuring Nichol Vineyard Syrah

Nichol Vineyard is a small farm winery which made a name for itself by being the first vineyard in Canada to plant Syrah grapes. Nichol Vineyard consistently produces a tasty Syrah that often has a "meaty" aroma and flavour. Thus it goes perfectly with this family favourite, the number one request for the homecoming dinner whenever one of the wandering offspring returns home.

Serves 4

INGREDIENTS

½ cup **Nichol Vineyard Syrah**

2 tbsp olive oil

1 large onion, finely chopped

1 cup carrot, grated

1½ cups mushrooms, chopped

1 lb ground bison (or lean beef)

4 garlic cloves, minced

1 tsp paprika

1 tsp chilli powder

1 small can tomato paste (5-6 oz)

1 cup water

1 tbsp molasses

1 tsp Worcestershire sauce

whole wheat French rolls or baguette

grated Parmesan or cheddar cheese

1. Heat oil over medium heat in a large saucepan that has a lid. Sauté onion, carrot and mushrooms until soft. Add bison (or beef) and crumble with a wooden spoon. Cook until no pink is left in the meat. Add garlic, paprika and chilli. Cook for 1 minute.

2. Stir in tomato paste, water, molasses and Worcestershire sauce. When blended, add the **Nichol Vineyard Syrah**. Increase to boiling point, lower heat, cover and gently simmer for 15 minutes. If too thick, add more wine.

3. While simmering, warm French rolls or baguette sliced to roll-sized pieces. Cut rolls lengthways, put on plate and cover with Sloppy Joe sauce.

4. If desired, sprinkle with cheese and broil quickly. Serve immediately with a simple green salad and the rest of the bottle of **Nichol Vineyard Syrah**. As an alternative option you may choose to serve "hamburger style" with a lid.

Nichol Vineyard

Location: 1285 Smethurst Road, Naramata, BC

Telephone: (250) 496-5962

Website and Email: www.nicholvineyard.com, nicholvineyard@shaw.ca

Wine Shop, Tours and Tastings: Open late-Jun - Thanksgiving, Tue-Sun 11 am-5pm. Also open Easter weekend, Okanagan Spring Wine Festival and May long weekend. Tours by appointment only.

Getting There: Follow Naramata Bench wineries signs northeast out of Penticton. This is the most northerly Naramata Bench winery, directly above the village of Naramata.

Highlights: The cosy wine shop has a spectacular view of Okanagan Lake and is just a stone's throw from the abandoned rail bed of the Kettle Valley Railway, perfect for walking, biking and picnics.

Syrah

Pronounced (see-rahh)

This wine is also known as Shiraz in South Africa, Australia and some British Columbian wineries with Australian influence. It is a wine with a long history. Many historians believe that the grape was originally grown in Southern Iran, near the village of Shiraz, before it was taken back to France by the crusaders, sometime between the 11th and 13th centuries. Other, less romantic historians contend that the grape has always been a native of France.

In France, the grape was originally grown in the Rhone Valley, where it was developed into the style of wine we have now come to love. It first made its appearance in British Columbia at Nichol Vineyard, where it is still growing today.

This variety buds rather late, but it ripens mid-season. The grape is thick-skinned and very dark. The wine is usually deep violet in colour and it often has aromas and flavours of blackberry, pepper, herbs and cinnamon. When the weather has been warm the wine is fruitier and cooler seasons give the wine more spicy aromas.

The wine pairs very well with heavy foods such as lamb, steak, Sloppy Joes, duck and game bird. It is also a guaranteed winner with just about anything that has been barbequed.

Pemberton Valley Elk Loin Medallions with Blueberry and Tantalus Sauce

Featuring Pemberton Valley Tantalus

The English word "tantalize" is derived from the Latin word "tantalus". In classical mythology Tantalus was so loved by the Gods that he was invited to dine with them, feasting on ambrosia and nectar in the halls of Olympia. This seductive wine is a Maréchal Foch blended with a little Merlot and Pinot Noir. It is aged in old French barrels for nine months and has a silky mouth feel and flavours of juicy sweet cherry, black plum, wild blackberry and chocolate, followed by a long elegant spicy and berry finish. This recipe created by Gary Faessler, works wondrously well with elk, venison or caribou.

Serves 4

INGREDIENTS

$^2/_3$ cup **Pemberton Valley Tantalus**

2 tbsp virgin olive oil

8 elk loin medallions (1 inch thick)

1 large garlic clove, minced

1 large shallot, minced

1 tbsp rosemary, finely chopped

1½ cups blueberries

¼ cup chilled unsalted butter, cubed

rosemary flowers to garnish

1. In a large skillet heat oil over medium-high heat. Sauté the medallions of loin on both sides, about 2 to 3 minutes per side. When finished rare to medium rare, transfer to an ovenproof dish and keep warm in a 150°F oven. Elk is so lean that choice cuts such as the loin require very little cooking. If cooked more than medium-rare the meat starts to become dry and tough.

2. Drain excess fat from the skillet and return it to the heat. Add garlic, rosemary, shallots and **Pemberton Valley Tantalus**. Deglaze the pan, stirring the liquid to loosen any browned bits. Cook over medium-high heat until sauce reduces by half. Add any pan juices that may have collected around the meat to the sauce.

3. Remove from heat and whisk in the butter, one piece at a time. Add blueberries and warm through. Divide the sauce evenly between 4 heated plates and place two elk medallions on top of the sauce. Garnish with rosemary flowers and serve with a glass of **Pemberton Valley Tantalus**.

Pemberton Valley Vineyard and Inn

Location: 1427 Collins Road, Pemberton, BC

Telephone: 1 (877) 444-5857

Website and Email: www.whistlerwine.com, bradner@whistlerwine.com

Wine Shop, Tours and Tastings: Open by appointment.

Getting There: Drive 30km north from Whistler into Pemberton. Turn right at the three-way stop by Bank of Scotia. Drive 500m and turn right onto Collins Road.

Highlights: Why not spend the night in luxury at the Inn? The vineyard planted in 1997, grows grapes carefully selected to suit the climate of the region.

Herder's Venison Steaks with Cranberry

Featuring Herder Merlot

Our 2003 Merlot was grown by three distinct vineyards throughout the Similkameen Valley. A hot summer produced ripe aromas and flavours of Bing cherry, blueberry, cedar and spice. The palate offers boysenberry, mocha, cherry, dried cranberry and butterscotch with a subtle finish.

Serves 4

INGREDIENTS

½ cup **Herder Merlot**

1 tbsp unsalted butter

2 garlic cloves, chopped

5 shallots, chopped

4 tbsp balsamic vinegar

10-12 oz cranberries

½ cup sugar

1 orange, wedged

2 whole cloves

1½ cups beef broth

1 tbsp sunflower oil

4 boneless venison steaks

1. Heat butter in a large skillet over low heat. Add chopped garlic and shallots and cook for 5 minutes or until softened. Add balsamic vinegar and cook for 3 minutes. Add cranberries, sugar, orange and cloves. Heat on high until sugar melts then reduce heat and simmer for 5 minutes.

2. Add broth and **Herder Merlot** and simmer for 10 minutes. Strain the juice through a sieve, extracting as much juice as possible. Discard the solids.

3. Heat oil in a large skillet over high heat. Add venison and cook for 3 minutes per side, until browned on the outside and cooked rare. Remove venison from the skillet and keep warm. Remove the fat from the pan, reheat sauce for 2 minutes and drizzle over the venison. Serve accompanied with a glass of **Herder Merlot**.

Herder Winery & Vineyards

Location: 716 Lowe Drive, Cawston, BC

Telephone/Fax: (250) 499-5595 / (250) 499-5531

Website and Email: www.herder.ca, info@herder.ca

Wine Shop, Tours and Tastings: Open May-Oct, daily 10am-6pm. Picnic area, wines by the glass, complimentary tasting.

Getting There: Heading east, the winery is 6.5km from Keremeos off of Highway 3. Heading west, it is 40km from Osoyoos off of Highway 3.

Highlights: Herder Winery & Vineyards specialises in producing small lots of vineyard specific wines. Enjoy a glass of wine while taking in a panoramic view from the valley floor.

Vegetarian

I made wine out of raisins so I wouldn't have to wait for it to age.

Steven Wright

Spinach and Basil Gnocchi

Garry Oaks Mushroom and Goat Cheese Parcels

Vegetarian Moussaka

Red Rooster's Goat Cheese and Red Pepper Penne

Township 7's Wild Mushroom Risotto

Broccoli and Sundried Tomato Pasta

Swiss Cheese Fondue

Spinach and Basil Gnocchi

Featuring BC Red Wine

Gnocchi (pronounced nyoh-kee) is a dish from Northern Italy with Germanic influence. The word "gnocchi" comes from the German word for "knuckle". The dish is made from potatoes and spinach both of which are grown right here in British Columbia. In fact there are over 10,000 hectares of farmland in the province devoted entirely to vegetables. This dish makes a great alternative to pasta.

Serves 6

INGREDIENTS

¾ cup **BC Red Wine**

2 lbs baking potatoes, unpeeled and cut into large pieces

6 oz fresh spinach, stems removed

2 tsp water

6 tbsp butter

1 large egg, beaten

1½ cups flour

2 tbsp olive oil

½ onion, chopped

2 tbsp tomato paste

¼ cup fresh basil, chopped

1 can chopped tomatoes (16 oz)

2 tsp sugar

salt and pepper to taste

Parmesan cheese

1. Place potatoes in a steamer until cooked. If you don't have a steamer, use a colander inside a large pot. Steaming should take 25-35 minutes, depending on the size of the potato pieces.

2. Over medium heat cook the spinach in a saucepan with the water for about 5-6 minutes, until it has completely wilted. Drain and pat dry. Chop it well. Remove potatoes from the steamer and peel and mash them while they are still hot. A potato ricer works best, but a fork will also do the job. Stir the spinach into the mashed potato.

3. Add the egg, butter and half of the flour to the mashed potato and spinach mixture. Mix together and then transfer to a floured surface. Using your hands knead the rest of the flour into the mixture making a big ball of soft dough. You want the dough to be fairly smooth and not sticky. The exact amount of flour used will be dependant on the amount of moisture in the potatoes, so be prepared to use a little more or less than the amounts we have indicated.

4. With floured hands, roll the dough into thin snakes about as thick as your finger. Cut the snakes into ¾ inch pieces. Press each piece of gnocchi with your finger so that there is a depression in the centre and the edges curl upwards. Place gnocchi on a tray in a single layer, cover and refrigerate while you make the sauce.

5. Heat the olive oil in a saucepan over medium heat. Add the onion and sauté for 5 minutes. Add the **BC Red Wine**, tomatoes, tomato paste, basil and sugar. Season with salt and pepper. Bring to a boil then reduce heat and allow to simmer for 25 minutes.

6. Bring a large pan of salted water to a boil. Add the gnocchi, letting them cook for 3-4 minutes until they rise. Remove with a slotted spoon, drain well and transfer to individual serving bowls. Serve topped with tomato basil sauce and Parmesan cheese.

Garry Oaks Mushroom and Goat Cheese Parcels

Featuring Garry Oaks Estate Pinot Noir

Made in the Burgundian style and aged in Garry Oak barrels, Garry Oaks Estate Pinot Noir is an elegant red wine. It has a classic earthy nose, flavours of dark berry and herb, and a touch of cinnamon and clove spice on the finish. When you make this recipe you are encouraged to use a variety of mushrooms, white, crimini, fresh shitake and portabellas. If you are using portabellas we advise you to remove the black gills from under the cap.

Serves 4

INGREDIENTS

¼ cup **Garry Oaks Estate Pinot Noir**

2 tbsp olive oil

1 large shallot, minced

1½ lbs mixed mushrooms, sliced

2 garlic cloves, crushed

¼ cup fresh parsley, chopped

½ tsp dried thyme

4 oz fresh Salt Spring Island goat cheese

8 sheets phyllo pastry, thawed

½ cup melted butter

salt and pepper to taste

1. Heat olive oil over low heat and sauté shallots for 3-4 minutes. Add sliced mushrooms and **Garry Oaks Estate Pinot Noir**, raise heat slightly and cook for about 10 minutes, stirring occasionally. Add garlic, parsley and thyme and cook for 2-3 minutes, stirring constantly. Put the cooked mixture in a food processor and process into a coarse paste. Transfer mixture to a bowl and mix in goat cheese. Add salt and pepper to taste. Set aside to cool.

2. Preheat oven to 400°F. Lay a phyllo pastry sheet on a work surface and brush with melted butter. Cover with a second sheet and brush again with butter. Divide filling into 4 portions. Spoon one portion on the bottom centre of each phyllo sheet then fold sheets over to form a rectangular parcel. Repeat this process to make 3 more parcels. Place seam down on baking sheet, brush top with melted butter and bake 25-30 minutes, until crisp and brown.

3. Enjoy this delicious meal with a glass of **Garry Oaks Estate Pinot Noir**.

Garry Oaks Winery

Location: 1880 Fulford-Ganges Road, Salt Spring Island, BC

Telephone/Fax: (250) 653-4687 / (250) 653-4426

Website and Email: www.garryoakswinery.com, info@garryoakswinery.com

Wine Shop, Tours and Tastings: Tasting room and wine shop open May-Thanksgiving; or by appointment. Call or email for hours. Group tours by appointment.

Getting There: Salt Spring is serviced by 3 ferries: from Tsawwassen, near Vancouver; from Swartz Bay, near Victoria; and from Crofton, near Duncan.

Highlights: Garry Oaks creates naturally small lots of original wines, classically inspired wines with a spirit of adventure.

Vegetarian Moussaka

Featuring BC Red Wine

This vegetarian take on the traditional Greek recipe requires a little effort but the result is well worth it.

Serves 8

INGREDIENTS

½ cup **BC Red Wine**

4 tbsp olive oil

1 cup onion, chopped

1 cup mushrooms, chopped

1 cup zucchini, chopped

1 tsp ground cinnamon

½ tsp dried oregano

½ cup parsley, chopped

2 tomatoes, chopped

½ cup tomato paste

2 eggplants cut into ½ inch slices

1½ cups milk

3 tbsp butter

3 tbsp flour

1 cup ricotta cheese

2 eggs, beaten

1 cup breadcrumbs

1 cup Parmesan cheese, grated

1. Heat 2 tbsp olive oil in a saucepan over medium-high heat. Sauté the onion for 4 minutes. Add mushrooms and zucchini and cook an additional 3 minutes. Add **BC Red Wine**, cinnamon, oregano, parsley, tomatoes and tomato paste. Bring to a boil. Reduce the heat to a simmer and let the liquid reduce until it is almost gone, stirring occasionally. This should take about 10-15 minutes. Remove from the heat and set aside.

2. Put the eggplant slices in a bowl. Add remaining olive oil and, using your hands, ensure that all of the slices are coated in the oil. Place the slices on a rack on top of a baking sheet under the broiler and cook for 4 minutes on each side or until browned. Save the leftover oil for later use.

3. Preheat the oven to 300°F. In a separate small saucepan heat the milk over medium-high heat until it starts to boil, then remove from the heat immediately and set aside. In a larger saucepan melt the butter over medium heat. As soon as it starts to froth, mix in the flour and whisk until it is well combined. Pour in the hot milk a little at a time and continue to whisk. Stir constantly until all of the milk is combined and the mixture has thickened. This should only take about 3 minutes. Remove from the heat and let it cool for a bit before stirring in the ricotta and then the eggs. Mix well.

4. Using oil leftover from the eggplant, grease a large rectangular baking dish. Sprinkle one-quarter of the breadcrumbs over the bottom of the dish. Next, add a layer of eggplant topped with a layer of the tomato mixture. Sprinkle with more breadcrumbs and top with some Parmesan cheese. Keep layering the ingredients until you run out. Finally, top with the ricotta mixture and bake for 1 hour. The top should be golden brown. After removing from the oven let the moussaka sit for 30 minutes before serving. Pour yourself a glass of **BC Red Wine** – you earned it

Foch

'Victory is a thing of the will' exclaimed General Ferdinand Foch, a famous French field marshal and commander of the Allied Forces during World War I. It is after General Foch that this grape variety has been named. The grape was actually created by a French Hybridiser, Eugene Kuhlman, who was greatly impressed by the actions of General Foch.

The full name of the grape is Maréchal Foch, although it is usually just shortened to Foch. This variety is an early ripening, high tonnage grape that is able to withstand harsh winter conditions. The variety was once a lot more widespread throughout British Columbia but many vines were pulled up in the late 1980s.

Some wineries in British Columbia have become masters of producing wonderful Foch wine. British Columbian consumers often see it as a specialty wine and it is in high demand. Foch goes well with roasted meat, duck, lamb and game.

Red Rooster's Goat Cheese and Red Pepper Penne

Featuring Red Rooster Merlot

The Red Rooster Merlot contains flavours of blackberries, soft plum, cherries and light toasty oak. It is a full-bodied, well-balanced wine that makes a wonderful accompaniment not only to meat, but also to rich tomato-based pasta dishes.

Serves 4

INGREDIENTS

½ cup **Red Rooster Merlot**
3 tbsp olive oil
4 shallots, chopped
2 garlic cloves, crushed
2 lbs Roma tomatoes, chopped
2 tbsp fresh basil, chopped

½ tsp dried oregano
2 red peppers, chopped
16 oz penne pasta, cooked al dente
6 oz goat cheese, chopped
salt and pepper to taste

1. Heat half of the olive oil in a saucepan over medium heat. Add shallots and garlic and sauté for 2-3 minutes. Add tomatoes and **Red Rooster Merlot**. Bring to a simmer for 12-15 minutes, stirring occasionally until desired sauce consistency is achieved. Add basil and oregano and simmer for an additional 5 minutes.

2. In a large pan heat remaining oil over medium heat. Add the peppers and sauté for 2-3 minutes. Add cooked pasta and sauce, heat through and stir, thoroughly coating the penne. Remove from the heat and add the goat cheese, tossing gently.

3. Serve immediately. This meal is perfectly accompanied by a glass of **Red Rooster Merlot**.

Red Rooster Winery

Location: 891 Naramata Road, Penticton, BC

Telephone/Fax: (250) 492-2424 / (250) 492-2400

Website and Email: www.redroosterwinery.com, redroosterwinery@shaw.ca

Wine Shop, Tours and Tastings: Wine shop open daily 10am-6pm. Winery tours at 1pm and 3pm, starting in beginning of May. Light lunches are served on the patio, starting in the beginning of May. For special events see the website.

Getting There: Off Highway 97 in Penticton, located only 5 minutes north of downtown Penticton on the east side of Okanagan Lake, on Naramata Road.

Highlights: Great lake and valley view from the all-new Red Rooster Winery. Sit on the patio and relax with a glass of wine and/or a light lunch. Taste award-winning wines in the gorgeous wine shop or explore the art gallery on the second floor. Visit one of the many events or hold your own event at the winery.

Township 7's Wild Mushroom Risotto

Featuring Township 7 Vineyards and Winery Chardonnay

This Chardonnay is 100% barrel fermented and aged in French and American oak barrels for six months. This wine displays pear, apple and citrus aromas and flavours accented by vanilla, spice and coconut. The wine displays harmonious integration of fruit and oak.

Serves 4

INGREDIENTS

½ cup **Township 7 Vineyards and Winery Chardonnay**

2½ tbsp olive oil

1 large white onion, diced

1 garlic clove, minced

1 tbsp fresh thyme, chopped

1 tbsp fresh oregano, chopped

2 cups Arborio rice

hot vegetable stock or water

1 cup each button, oyster, shitake mushrooms, chopped

¼ cup shaved Parmesan cheese

salt and white pepper to taste

1. In a saucepan over medium heat sauté onion and garlic in 1½ tbsp of olive oil for 6 minutes or until translucent, stirring frequently. Add the fresh herbs and stir for an additional minute. Add rice and 4 cups of stock or water. Stir constantly until rice has absorbed most of the liquid. Continue adding additional liquid in small amounts until the rice is cooked al dente (still has a slight crunch to it). Set rice aside, off the heat.

2. Sauté the mushrooms in remaining olive oil in a separate pan over medium heat. Add rice to the sautéed mushrooms then add **Township 7 Vineyards and Winery Chardonnay**. Stir for 1 minute over low heat. The rice should have a creamy texture at this stage – add a small amount of liquid if necessary.

3. Season to taste with salt, white pepper, Parmesan cheese and butter. This risotto is perfect served with shaved Parmesan, French bread and **Township Vineyards and Winery Chardonnay**.

Township 7 Vineyards and Winery

Location 1: 21152 – 16th Avenue, Langley, BC

Location 2: 1450 McMillan Avenue, Penticton, BC

Telephone: Langley (604) 532-1766 **Penticton** (250) 770-1743

Website and Email: www.township7.com, wine@township7.com

Wine Shop, Tours and Tastings: Langley: Jan by appointment; Feb–Jun and Sep-Nov, Thu-Sun (tastings on weekends). July, Aug, Dec, open daily 11am-6pm. Penticton: Open mid-May – mid-Oct. Call for details.

Getting There: Langley – 45 minutes southeast of Vancouver. Look for signs along Highway 1 east of Vancouver or Highway 99 south of Vancouver. **Penticton** – East of Penticton on the Naramata Bench; refer to website or call for specific details.

Highlights: This young winery has won many high profile awards including "BC Winery to Watch" and "Canadian White Wine of the Year".

Broccoli and Sundried Tomato Pasta

Featuring BC Pinot Blanc

It is easy to see why this dish can quickly become a family favourite. The beans give the dish a great texture and are very healthy to boot!

Serves 4

INGREDIENTS

1½ cups **BC Pinot Blanc**	½ tsp red pepper flakes
1 cup sundried tomatoes	2 cups cooked white beans (or 1 can)
2 tbsp olive oil	¼ cup fresh basil, chopped
2 garlic cloves, minced	16 oz pasta
1 medium onion, chopped	salt and pepper to taste
3½ cups broccoli, chopped	shavings fresh parmesan for garnish

1. Cut the sundried tomatoes into strips. Put them in a bowl and cover with **BC Pinot Blanc**, soaking for 1 hour.

2. Heat oil in a large frying pan over medium heat. Add onion and garlic and sauté for 5 minutes. Add broccoli and red pepper flakes, stirring occasionally for an additional 3-4 minutes. Add sundried tomato mixture, beans and basil. Bring to a boil and then reduce to a simmer for 10-12 minutes.

3. Cook pasta al dente, according to the instructions on the package, then divide it among 4 deep pasta bowls. Top the pasta with the sauce and shavings of Parmesan cheese and serve immediately with a glass of **BC Pinot Blanc**.

Swiss Cheese Fondue

Featuring BC Dry White Wine

The word "fondue" is a derivative of the French word "fondre", which means "to melt". After a day on BC's world-class ski slopes there is nothing better than enjoying a warm dish like this in the company of a few close friends.

Serves 4

INGREDIENTS

2 cups **BC Dry White Wine**

2 garlic cloves

1 tbsp lemon juice

1 lb Swiss cheese, grated

3 tbsp flour

3 tbsp cherry brandy

2 loaves of crusty bread, cubed

1. Rub a pot well with garlic cloves and pour in the **BC Dry White Wine**. Set over medium heat. Just before the wine boils add the lemon juice.

2. Start adding the grated cheese one handful at a time, stirring continuously.

3. In a separate bowl mix the cherry brandy and flour, then add this to the cheese mixture and stir well. Transfer to a fondue pot.

4. To serve, put the fondue pot over the burner in the centre of the table. Using skewers spear the bread and dip it into the fondue, swirling to coat.

Side Dishes

God made only water, but man made wine.

Victor Hugo, 1802-1885

Risi e Bisi Cheesi

Mixed Mushroom Medley

Red Swiss Chard with Garlic and Wine

Scalloped Potatoes with Goat Cheese and Herbs

Baby Carrots Baked in Wine, Cumin and Thyme

Eggplant Parmigiana

Green Beans and Mushrooms

Garlic Broccoli with a Kick

Oven Roasted Veggies

Risi e Bisi Cheesi

Featuring BC White Wine

"Risi e Bisi" is Italian for "rice and peas". It is a traditional Venetian dish that was once only prepared on feast days. This version is very simple to prepare. If you do not want to use frozen peas, cook some fresh peas in salted water beforehand.

Serves 4

INGREDIENTS

¾ cup **BC White Wine**

2 tbsp olive oil

1 garlic clove, chopped

1 onion, chopped

1 cup Arborio rice

3½ cups chicken or vegetable stock

¼ cup Parmesan cheese, grated

1 cup frozen small peas

1 tbsp flat leaf parsley, chopped

salt and pepper to taste

1. Heat oil in a medium-sized saucepan over medium heat. Add garlic and onion. Stir and sauté for 3 minutes before adding the rice. Continue stirring for 1 minute.

2. Add the **BC White Wine**, stir for 1 minute or until the wine has completely disappeared, then add the first cup of stock. When the liquid is absorbed add another ½ cup of stock. You must keep stirring – it should take about 20-25 minutes before all of the stock is used. Add the peas just before the rice is done. It should be cooked all'onda, meaning moist and creamy rather than firm.

3. Add the cheese, parsley, salt and pepper and stir though until the peas are soft and juicy. Remove from heat and serve.

Mixed Mushroom Medley

Featuring BC Pinot Noir

There is nothing like the divine flavour of freshly cooked mushrooms. Here we get the best BC has to offer with a combination of freshly picked produce and heavenly Pinot Noir. This is a dish you will make again and again.

Serves 4

INGREDIENTS

¾ cup **BC Pinot Noir**

1½ lbs mixed mushrooms (wild, porcini, oyster, morel, etc.)

1 cup vegetable stock

2 tbsp fresh parsley, chopped

4 garlic cloves, crushed

2 tbsp fresh thyme, chopped

¼ cup whipping cream

½ cup olive oil

1 cup Parmesan Cheese, grated

salt and pepper to taste

1. If using dried mushrooms then soak them in warm water for 1½ hours before use. Reserve the liquid they were re-hydrated in. Separate the mushroom heads from the stems. Chop the stems into fine pieces and set aside. Slice the heads into thick slices and set aside.

2. In a small saucepan combine **BC Pinot Noir** and stock. If you have used dried mushrooms add 1 cup of the water they were re-hydrated in. Bring to a boil and add the stems, parsley, garlic, thyme, cream and pepper. Simmer until liquid is reduced to gravy.

3. Divide chopped mushroom heads into 4 piles. Heat one-quarter of the olive oil in a large frying pan over medium heat and then add one pile of mushrooms. Sauté the mushrooms for about 6-7 minutes or until cooked. Repeat using remaining oil and mushrooms, one pile at a time.

4. When all of the mushrooms are cooked, return them all to the pan and add sauce. Cook for a further 5 minutes.

5. Serve immediately, topped with Parmesan cheese. This dish is divine served with a glass of **BC Pinot Noir**.

Red Swiss Chard with Garlic and Wine

Featuring BC White Wine

Swiss Chard is probably the healthiest vegetable you could ever eat. It is jam-packed full of vitamins and goodness. Research has shown that this vegetable can even help prevent emphysema, making it a wise choice for smokers. Having said that, a lot of people hate the taste of Swiss chard. We have come up with this recipe to ensure that the vegetable not only gets eaten, but it could actually become a household favourite.

Serves 4

INGREDIENTS

½ cup **BC White Wine**

2 tbsp vegetable oil

4 garlic cloves, crushed

1 lb red Swiss chard, chopped

salt and pepper to taste

1. Heat the oil over medium heat in a large pan that has a lid. Add garlic and sauté for 30 seconds. Add Swiss chard, **BC White Wine**, salt and pepper. Cover and cook for about 10 minutes or until tender.

Scalloped Potatoes with Goat Cheese and Herbs

Featuring BC Dry White Wine

This is a delicious side dish that is perfect for serving with baked meals as you can throw this dish in the oven at the same time.

Serves 8

INGREDIENTS

¾ cup **BC Dry White Wine**

1 cup vegetable stock

1¼ cups whipping cream

½ cup onion, chopped

½ tsp salt

1 tsp dried oregano

1 tbsp dried thyme

1 tbsp dried rosemary

1 log of goat cheese (10-12 oz)

3 lbs potatoes, peeled and sliced thin

½ tbsp butter

1. Preheat the oven to 400°F. Mix **BC Dry White Wine**, stock, cream, onion, salt and dried herbs together in a large saucepan over medium-high heat. Bring to a simmer and then crumble in half of the goat cheese and whisk the mixture smooth. Add the potatoes to the saucepan and simmer for 3-4 minutes.

2. Use the butter to grease an ovenproof dish. Transfer the mixture from the pan to the dish. Cover with aluminium foil and bake in the oven for 15 minutes. Remove the foil and continue to bake another 45 minutes until potatoes are soft and the mixture is thick.

3. Crumble the remaining goat cheese evenly over the potatoes and let them bake another 5 minutes. Remove from the oven to cool for 10-15 minutes before serving.

Baby Carrots Baked in Wine, Cumin and Thyme

Featuring BC White Wine

The Greeks used thyme as an emblem of courage and the Romans used it to cure melancholy. Cumin has been used since biblical times for its calming digestive properties. Carrots are Bugs Bunny's favourite food. Here they are combined in a baked dish that goes well with just about anything. The wonderful flavours of the cumin and thyme are divine with this wine and butter sauce over tender baby carrots.

Serves 4

INGREDIENTS

¾ cup **BC White Wine**

1 lb baby carrots

½ cup loosely packed fresh thyme leaves, chopped

½ tsp cumin seeds, crushed

4 tbsp butter

salt and pepper to taste

1. Preheat the oven to 425°F. Combine **BC White Wine**, carrots, thyme, cumin and butter in a small, shallow baking dish. Add salt and pepper to taste.

2. Cover the dish with aluminium foil and bake for 50 minutes to 1 hour, until carrots are juicy and tender.

Eggplant Parmigiana

Featuring BC Red Wine

Eggplant is not as popular in North America as it is in the rest of the world. This is a tragedy because so many wonderful dishes can be made with this relation of the potato, tomato and pepper. This recipe is probably our all-time favourite side dish.

Serves 4

INGREDIENTS

½ cup **BC Red Wine**

¼ cup and 1 tsp olive oil

1 egg, beaten

1 tbsp milk

½ cup dried breadcrumbs

¼ tsp salt

1 eggplant, sliced into ½ inch slices

2 garlic cloves, crushed

¾ cup tomato paste

6 oz mozzarella cheese, thinly sliced

1 cup Parmesan cheese, grated

1. Preheat the oven to 400°F. Grease the bottom of a large baking dish with a little olive oil.

2. In a bowl or dish combine the beaten egg with the milk. Fill a separate plate with breadcrumbs and salt and mix well. Dip the slices of eggplant into the egg mixture and then coat with the breadcrumbs. Lay the slices on the greased baking dish in a single layer. Drizzle the remaining olive oil, except 1 reserved tsp, over them, making sure to get some on each slice.

3. Place the dish in the oven for 15 minutes, turn the slices over and bake for another 15 minutes, until golden brown on each side.

4. In a small saucepan over medium heat sauté the garlic in 1 tsp of olive oil. Add the **BC Red Wine** and tomato paste and simmer for 10-15 minutes.

5. When the eggplant is done, remove the baking dish from the oven. Top each eggplant slice with a generous amount of tomato sauce and a slice of mozzarella. Finally, cover the whole dish with Parmesan cheese and return to the oven for about 15-20 minutes. Let it sit for 5 minutes before serving.

Green Beans and Mushrooms

Featuring BC White Wine

Green beans are delicious served in this traditional French dish. When shopping for the freshest green beans you should be looking for young, long pods and the sides should be starting to bulge with the juicy beans inside. If you snap the bean, there should be a pop and the inside should be relatively free of fibres.

Serves 4

INGREDIENTS

½ cup **BC White Wine**

½ tsp vegetable oil

1 garlic clove, finely chopped

¼ cup onion, chopped

½ cup chicken or vegetable stock

1 tsp oregano

2½ cups fresh green beans, cut into 1 inch pieces

1½ cups fresh mushrooms, sliced

salt and pepper to taste

1. Heat vegetable oil in a pan over medium-high heat. Add garlic and onion and sauté for 3 minutes while stirring. Add stock and simmer for 1 minute.

2. Add **BC White Wine**, oregano, mushrooms and green beans. Cover and bring to a boil then simmer for 2 minutes. Remove cover and continue simmering until beans are tender. This will only take a couple of minutes.

3. Using a slotted spoon, remove the beans, mushrooms and garlic and transfer to a serving dish or to individual plates. Add salt and pepper to taste. Keep reducing the sauce and pour a little over top of the beans for extra flavour.

Garlic Broccoli with a Kick

Featuring BC White Wine

Broccoli is rich in vitamins and high in fibre. It is also said to contain as much calcium, gram for gram, as milk! When choosing broccoli, look for heads with tight, compact bud clusters that are an even, dark colour. The stems should be easy to pierce with your fingernail. If the stems are hard and dry, or the bud clusters are open or yellowing, keep looking.

Serves 4

INGREDIENTS

½ cup **BC White Wine**

¼ cup olive oil

3 garlic cloves, sliced

¾ lb broccoli, cut into florets

½ tsp fresh lemon juice

1 tbsp dried chilli flakes

1. Heat the olive oil in a large sauté pan over medium heat until hot. Add the garlic and broccoli, stirring frequently. Slowly add the **BC White Wine** throughout the cooking process, about 10 minutes. As the liquid evaporates, add more. Add the lemon juice with the last of the **BC White Wine**. The broccoli is cooked when the stems are tender.

2. Finally, add the dried chilli flakes. Remember to make sure that your guests like chilli – or adjust the amount and only add a little. Stir thoroughly and then transfer to a serving platter or individual plates.

Auxerrois

PRONOUNCED — (OX-AIR-WAH)

THE AUXERROIS GRAPE ORIGINATES IN THE ALSACE REGION OF FRANCE, WHICH
BORDERS GERMANY. THERE IT IS OFTEN USED AS A BLENDING GRAPE, WHERE
IT IS USUALLY MIXED WITH PINOT BLANC.

MOST HISTORIANS AND WINE BUFFS AGREE THAT IT WAS GEORGE HEISS OF
GRAY MONK ESTATE WHO FIRST IMPORTED THE GRAPE TO BRITISH COLUMBIA IN
THE EARLY 1970S. THE GRAPE IS GROWN THROUGHOUT BRITISH COLUMBIA
AND DOES WELL IN THE MORE TEMPERATE CLIMATE OF VANCOUVER ISLAND, AS
WELL AS THE VARYING CLIMATE OF THE OKANAGAN.

SOME WINERIES, INCLUDING BRITISH COLUMBIA'S GRAY MONK ESTATE, PREFER
TO CALL THE GRAPE PINOT AUXERROIS, WHILE OTHERS PREFER THE SHORTER
NAME. THE WINE HAS WELL-DEFINED AROMAS AND FLAVOURS RANGING FROM
GREEN APPLES AND CITRUS TO PEACHES AND RHUBARB.

THIS WINE IS ONE OF THE FEW WINES THAT PAIRS EASILY WITH MOST SALADS. IT
ALSO GOES WELL WITH FISH AND POULTRY.

Oven Roasted Veggies

Featuring BC White Wine

A full compliment of delicious oven-roasted vegetables make up this roasted veggie platter that can accompany all sorts of dishes. It can even be a meal on its own.

Serves 8

INGREDIENTS

¼ cup **BC White Wine**	2 tbsp olive oil
3 medium parsnips, cut into chunks	2 sprigs fresh rosemary
2 large carrots, cut into chunks	8 Brussels sprouts, halved
8 large potatoes, quartered	2½ tbsp butter
2 turnips, cut into large chunks	1 tbsp fresh flat leaf parsley, chopped
8 garlic cloves, unpeeled	salt and pepper to taste

1. Preheat the oven to 375°F. Put parsnips, carrots, potatoes, turnips and garlic in a plastic bag. Add 1 tbsp olive oil and coat the vegetables. Transfer the oiled vegetables to a baking dish. Rub the vegetables with rosemary then add the rosemary sprigs to the pan. Roast for 25 minutes.

2. Meanwhile, bring a saucepan full of salted water to a boil. Drop in the Brussels sprouts for 2 minutes. Drain well and add the sprouts to the vegetables in the oven. Drizzle remaining olive oil over the vegetables. Sprinkle them with salt and pepper, pour in the **BC White Wine** and dab dollops of butter over them. Roast for another 15 minutes

3. Remove the vegetables from the oven, sprinkle with chopped parsley and mix through before serving. Divide the veggies amongst the plates or place them in a serving dish in the centre of the table.

Marinades

The peoples of the Mediterranean began to emerge from barbarism
when they learnt to cultivate the olive and the vine.

Thucydides, Greek Historian, 5th century BC

Peller Estates Sweet and Spiced Chicken Marinade

White Honey Mustard Marinade

Red Honey Mustard Marinade

Syrah Marinade

Lemon and Herb Marinade

BBQ Marinade

Teriyaki Marinade

Peller Estates Sweet and Spiced Chicken Marinade

Featuring Peller Estates Trinity Icewine

In 1961 European winemaker Andrew Peller fulfilled his lifelong dream to create premium quality wines with the inception of Andres wines. Today they produce premium wines that proudly bear the Peller family name. John Parsons, Executive Chef at the Peller Estates Winery Restaurant has created this wonderful BBQ recipe using the delicious Trinity Icewine.

Serves 6

INGREDIENTS

1 cup **Peller Estates Trinity Icewine**

2 tbsp fresh tarragon

2 cups low-fat yoghurt

1 tsp red chilli, finely chopped

1 tbsp verjus

6 whole chicken breasts

1. In a mixing bowl, combine the **Peller Estates Trinity Icewine**, tarragon, yoghurt, chilli and verjus until well blended. Pour over chicken breasts and chill in the refrigerator overnight.

2. Remove the chicken breast from the marinade and grill on a barbeque. Season with salt and pepper and serve. After eating the chicken try a glass of **Peller Estates Trinity Icewine** for dessert.

Peller Estates

Location: 2120 Vintner Street, Port Moody, BC

Telephone: (604) 937-3411

Website: www.andreswines.com

Wine Shop, Tours and Tastings: Open year-round, Mon-Fri 8am-4pm

Getting There: Not far from Vancouver, the winery is located in Port Moody. Follow St Johns Street and turn onto Douglas Street heading towards the water. Turn left onto Vintner Street.

Highlights: Peller makes a variety of wonderful wines to suit all occasions and budgets.

White Honey Mustard Marinade

Featuring BC Dry White Wine

This marinade is perfect for chicken or pork. You can also use it for salmon but reduce the marinating time to around 20-25 minutes and baste the fish with the mixture while cooking.

Makes about 2 cups

INGREDIENTS

1 cup **BC Dry White Wine**

½ cup Dijon mustard

¾ cup olive oil

¼ cup honey

1 garlic clove, crushed

2 tbsp soy sauce

1. Combine all the ingredients in a bowl. Add meat, ensure it is completely covered and refrigerate for at least 3 hours.

Red Honey Mustard Marinade

Featuring BC Cabernet Sauvignon

This marinade is great for lamb. Try using different herbs such as dill, tarragon or basil for completely different results. You can substitute the wine with your favourite BC red for a different flavour.

Makes about 1½ cups

INGREDIENTS

1 cup **BC Cabernet Sauvignon**
½ cup extra virgin olive oil
1½ tsp Dijon mustard

2 garlic cloves, minced
2 tbsp honey
1½ tbsp fresh rosemary, chopped

1. Combine all the ingredients in a saucepan and bring to a boil. Reduce heat and simmer for 5 minutes, stirring occasionally. Refrigerate the marinade before adding the meat. Marinade the meat for 3 hours to overnight before cooking.

Cabernet Sauvignon

Pronounced (ca-burr-nay soh-vin-yon)

Cabernet Sauvignon, or "Cab Sav" as it is affectionately termed by some wine lovers, is one of the most popular red wines in the world. The grape can be traced back to the Médoc district in the Bordeaux region of France, where it is still prominent today.

The grape is a fairly new addition to British Columbia and it really made its debut in the early 1990s. The grapes often do not become ripe until later in the season, which in British Columbia can cause some problems. Still, some remarkable examples of Cabernet Sauvignon continue to be produced in the province.

Cabernet Sauvignon wines are fantastic for aging. Very often "good" wines will become "great" wines after cellaring. Cabernet Sauvignon also blends remarkably well and when combined with Merlot, it becomes a little mellower without losing its character.

Cabernet Sauvignon pairs wonderfully with steak, pasta, tomato-based sauces, dark meats, duck, blue cheese and dark chocolate. Known to many as "the king of red wine" this variety is unlikely to lose its throne anytime soon.

Syrah Marinade

Featuring BC Syrah

This marinade is wonderful for pork, beef and lamb. Only make this amount if you are cooking for a large group, or if you want to save some for later.

Makes about 5 cups

INGREDIENTS

1 cup **BC Syrah**

2 tsp minced horseradish

2 cups ketchup

2 cups olive oil

4 garlic cloves, minced

1 tbsp oregano

1 tbsp Worcestershire sauce

2 tbsp shallots, minced

2 tbsp fresh parsley, chopped

1 bay leaf

1 tbsp rosemary, chopped

1. Combine all of the ingredients in a large bowl or plastic container. Meat should be marinated overnight for best results. If this is not possible, then allow at least 4 hours.

Lemon and Herb Marinade

Featuring BC White Wine

This is a great marinade for fish, lamb, pork and veal. You should never pierce meat that you are going to marinade. It does not help the flavour to penetrate and actually creates an escape for the juices of the meat when you cook it. By piercing it you actually end up with drier meat.

Makes about 1½ cups

INGREDIENTS

½ cup **BC White Wine**

½ cup lemon juice

½ cup olive oil

2 garlic cloves, finely chopped

½ tsp dried rosemary

½ tsp dried oregano

½ tsp dried thyme

1 tsp lemon zest, grated

1 tbsp parsley, chopped

salt and pepper to taste

1. Combine everything in a bowl and mix well. Place the meat in the marinade at least a couple of hours before cooking. If you are marinating fish you should not leave it so long or the lemon juice will start to cook the fish before it gets into the pan.

BBQ Marinade

Featuring BC Red Wine

This marinade is great for barbeques as it gives a special added touch to anything you throw on the grill. It also works very well as a basting sauce. Try going to a barbeque with a bottle of this secret basting sauce - everyone will be asking you what's in it. We prepare it the night before the BBQ and let it sit in a sealed container at room temperature.

Makes about 2½ cups

INGREDIENTS

1 cup **BC Red Wine**

½ cup white wine vinegar

½ cup olive oil

¾ cup chives, finely chopped

1 cup parsley, finely chopped

½ tsp salt

1 tbsp soy sauce

1 tsp black pepper

1. Just combine all the ingredients. That's it! Done! It makes a great marinade or basting sauce for all meats, poultry, fish, or just about anything you could ever want to BBQ.

Teriyaki Marinade

Featuring BC Red Wine

The term "teriyaki" in Japan means something quite different from the teriyaki we know in North America. In Japan it refers to a sweet-sour sauce that is applied to meat during the last stage of cooking. "Teri" means shine or gloss and "yaki" refers to cooked meat. In North America teriyaki means meat marinated in a teriyaki sauce mixture, which is the recipe we have provided here.

Makes about 2½ cups

INGREDIENTS

¾ cup **BC Red Wine**

1½ cups Kikkoman soy sauce

1 piece ginger grated (1 inch)

1 garlic clove, crushed

½ cup brown sugar

1 tsp sesame oil

1. Combine all the ingredients and marinate the meat. Beef can be marinated overnight, chicken for about 2-3 hours and fish for about 30 minutes.

Sauces & Condiments

It is, of course, entirely possible to cook without using wine. It is also possible to wear suits and dresses made out of gunny sacks, but who wants to?

Morrison Wood (1949) 'With a Jug of Wine'

Lotusland's Tomato Mushroom Rosé Pasta Sauce

Traditional Bolognese Sauce

Wine and Cheese Sauce

The Very Best Béarnaise Sauce

Dill and Mustard Beurre Blanc

Creamy White Wine Sauce

The Ridge Restaurant's Rosemary Apple Chutney

Wellbrook's Cranberry Orange Chutney

Bonaparte Bend Wine Jelly

Lotusland's Tomato Mushroom Rosé Pasta Sauce

Featuring Lotusland Merlot

Celebrity Chef Dez (Gordon Desormeaux) has come up with this recipe using the 2002 Lotusland Merlot. The wine is deep crimson in colour and has aromas of black cherry with a hint of white pepper on the nose. The flavours are fruitbomb, cherry, plum and a hint of anise and chocolate. It has a smooth finish and will continue to evolve in the bottle.

Makes 4 cups

INGREDIENTS

1 cup **Lotusland Merlot**

4 tbsp olive oil

1 medium carrot, finely diced

1 large celery stalk, finely diced

½ medium white onion, finely diced

6 garlic cloves, crushed

20 medium button mushrooms, sliced

1 can diced tomatoes (28 oz)

1 tbsp plus 1 tsp white sugar

¼ cup 35% whipping cream

salt and black pepper to taste

1. Heat a heavy bottomed pot over medium heat and add 2 tbsp of olive oil. Add carrot, celery, onion and garlic. Gently season with salt and pepper. Sweat until soft but not brown, about 2-3 minutes, stirring frequently.

2. Add mushrooms and the remaining olive oil, along with another sprinkle of salt if necessary. Gently cook for about 2-3 minutes, stirring occasionally. Add the can of tomatoes. Increase heat to high until liquid is almost gone. Gradually lower heat from high to medium-high, watching closely and stirring frequently, about 10-15 minutes.

3. Add the **Lotusland Merlot** and reduce again over medium-high heat, stirring occasionally and gradually lowering heat to medium, about 10 minutes. Stir in the sugar and cream and remove from the heat. Season to taste.

4. Serve with your favourite pasta. Garnish with fresh parsley and grated Parmesan cheese.

Lotusland Vineyards

Location: 28450 King Road (16th Avenue), Abbotsford, BC

Telephone / Fax: (604) 847-4188 / (604) 856-8299

Website and Email: www.lotuslandvineyards.com, info@lotuslandvineyards.com

Wine Shop, Tours and Tastings: Boutique is open Apr-Sep, Wed-Mon 11am-6pm; Oct-Mar, Thu-Sun 11am-5pm; or by happenchance. Tours by appointment.

Getting There: From Highway 1 turn south on Highway 13 (264th Street) and then east on 16th Avenue. Drive for 4km and then turn in-between the stone pillars.

Highlights: A 100% organic vineyard since day one. All fruit is estate-grown in the Mt Lehman area. First winery to exclusively use Stelvin closures – no cork taint!

Traditional Bolognese Sauce

Featuring BC Dry White Wine

This is a traditional recipe based on the popular sauce from the city of Bologna, in Northern Italy. This recipe takes a long time to cook so make sure that you have time before you start. As millions of satisfied Italians will testify, the results are well worth the wait.

Serves 6

INGREDIENTS

1 cup **BC Dry White Wine**	¾ lb lean ground beef
3 tbsp olive oil	½ cup milk
4 tbsp butter	1 pinch of nutmeg
2 tbsp onion, chopped	1 can of tomatoes (14 oz)
2 tbsp celery, chopped	salt and pepper to taste
2 tbsp carrot, chopped	

1. Heat the oil and butter over medium heat in a deep, heavy skillet. Add chopped onion and sauté for 4-5 minutes until just translucent. Add carrots and celery and cook for an additional 2 minutes.

2. Add the beef, crumbling it into the skillet with a wooden spoon. As soon as the meat loses its pinkish appearance, add the **BC Dry White Wine**. Turn up the heat to medium-high and stir until the wine has evaporated.

3. Turn the heat back down to medium and add the milk and nutmeg. Continue stirring until the milk has evaporated. Add the tomatoes and stir well. As soon as the sauce begins to boil, reduce the heat to the lowest possible simmer. Simmer for 4-5 hours. Stir occasionally and add salt and pepper to taste.

4. This sauce is fantastic over hot pasta, topped with slivers of fresh Parmesan cheese. Leftover sauce can be frozen or stored in the refrigerator for up to 3 days. Just reheat and serve.

Deglaze

If you are looking for a simple but tasty sauce to accompany your dish, deglazing the pan is often the easiest way.

When you finish cooking meat or fish, remove it from the pan and add a small amount of wine: red or white, depending on the dish. Then, using a wooden spoon, scrape up the brown bits that are stuck to the bottom. These will give the sauce flavour. Let the wine reduce a little over the heat and "voila", a perfect sauce every time.

This type of sauce, although simple, is a most delicious accompaniment to the food you have just cooked. It must be noted that this will not work if drippings on the bottom of the pan are burnt.

Wine and Cheese Sauce

Featuring BC White Wine

This cheese sauce is easy to prepare and is delicious served with vegetables, pasta, chicken or fish. You can be creative and use a variety of cheeses to change the sauce completely.

Makes 2 cups

INGREDIENTS

½ cup **BC White Wine**

1½ cups milk

4 tbsp butter

3 tbsp flour

1 dash cayenne pepper (optional)

¾ cup cheese, grated

salt to taste

1. In a small saucepan, bring the milk to a simmer.

2. In a separate saucepan, melt the butter over medium heat. Add the flour and stir until well combined.

3. Slowly add the hot milk to the flour/butter mixture, stirring constantly until the sauce thickens. Add the **BC White Wine**, cayenne pepper and salt and continue to simmer and stir over a very low heat for about 10 minutes.

4. Add the grated cheese and stir well. Remove from the heat when cheese is melted through.

The Very Best Béarnaise Sauce

Featuring BC White Wine

Béarnaise sauce makes an elegant accompaniment to so many dishes, including grilled salmon, roast lamb, steak, venison, moose and even scallops and lobsters. Most people think this sauce comes from the French city of Béarn, but that is not the case. It was created in the early 1800s by a chef in Île-de-France who worked at a restaurant called Pavillon Henry IV, named after the famous French king. As King Henry was born in Béarn, the chef named the sauce Béarnaise.

Makes about 1½ cups

INGREDIENTS

½ cup **BC White Wine**

¼ medium onion, finely chopped

1½ tsp dried tarragon

½ tsp black pepper

1 cup butter

6 egg yolks

2½ tbsp tarragon vinegar

1. In a pan over medium heat combine **BC White Wine**, onion, tarragon and black pepper. Simmer until the liquid in the pan is reduced to about one-quarter.

2. In a separate pan melt the butter and bring it to a gentle simmer.

3. Put the egg yolks and tarragon vinegar in a food processor or a blender. If you use a blender, make sure to use one that has a hole in the lid where you can add ingredients.

4. When the butter is melted, turn on the food processor or the blender and slowly pour in the melted butter. Then add the wine and onion reduction. Let it blend for 10 seconds.

5. Serve warm over a juicy steak or a fillet of salmon; the options are limitless. Transfer any unused mixture to a non-metallic bowl, cover and refrigerate. This sauce will keep for up to 3 days in the refrigerator. Make sure you reheat it gently or you might get scrambled eggs. We recommend using a double boiler.

Dill and Mustard Beurre Blanc

Featuring BC White Wine

This delicious version of beurre blanc is perfect for salmon, but it has a lot more uses than that. It also goes very well with scallops, chicken, ham, veal and beef.

Makes 1½ cups

INGREDIENTS

1 cup **BC White Wine**	2 tbsp whole grain Dijon mustard
½ cup white wine vinegar	1 tbsp fresh dill, chopped
4 shallots, finely chopped	1 tsp honey
¾ cup chilled butter, cubed	salt and pepper to taste

1. Combine the **BC White Wine**, vinegar and shallots in a small saucepan and bring to a boil. Stir constantly until liquid is reduced by about one-third. Reduce heat to low.

2. One by one, whisk in the cubes of butter. You want the sauce to be just below simmering temperature, so take it off the heat for a few seconds if it starts to simmer.

3. Finally, whisk in the mustard, dill, honey, salt and pepper.

Creamy White Wine Sauce

Featuring BC White Wine

This easy to prepare white sauce offers endless possibilities, served with fish, poultry and gratin dishes; or as the basis of many other sauces. If the milk is hot when you add it to the flour and butter mixture there should not be any lumps. If for some reason there are lumps, just put it into a blender for a few seconds.

Makes 2 cups

INGREDIENTS

½ cup **BC White Wine**

1½ cups milk

4 tbsp butter

3 tbsp flour

1 dash cayenne pepper (optional)

salt to taste

1. In a small saucepan bring the milk to a simmer.

2. In a separate saucepan melt the butter over medium heat. Add the flour, stirring until combined.

3. Slowly add the hot milk to the flour/butter mixture, stirring constantly until the sauce thickens. Add the **BC White Wine** and continue to simmer and stir over very low heat for about 10 minutes. Season to taste with salt and cayenne pepper.

The Ridge Restaurant's Rosemary Apple Chutney

Featuring Raven Ridge Fuji Iced Cider

Raven Ridge Cidery has combined traditional cider-making and the new innovations of icewine production to create an outstanding new line of iced apple ciders.

INGREDIENTS

1 cup **Raven Ridge Fuji Iced Cider**

2 tbsp extra virgin olive oil

1 white onion, diced

4 garlic cloves, minced

1 tbsp ground coriander

1 tsp ground cumin

1 sprig rosemary, chopped

1 cup apple cider vinegar

1 cup honey

6 large Fuji apples, peeled, cored and chopped

½ cup cold butter, cubed

salt and pepper to taste

1. Heat oil in a medium-sized saucepan over medium heat. Add onion, garlic, coriander and cumin. Cook until ingredients are juicy and tender. Add rosemary, vinegar, honey and **Raven Ridge Fuji Iced Cider** and bring to a simmer.

2. Add chopped apple and continue cooking until apple becomes tender. Remove from the heat and add butter one cube at a time, stirring evenly to melt the butter.

3. This is delicious served with chicken or pork, or as a condiment for cheese and crackers. It is also awesome when puréed and served on potato pancakes! Accompany with a glass of **Raven Ridge Fuji Iced Cider.**

Raven Ridge Cidery Inc.

Location: Kelowna Land & Orchard, 3002 Dunster Road, Kelowna, BC

Telephone: (250) 763-1091

Website and Email: www.k-l-o.com, klo@k-l-o.com

Wine Shop, Tours and Tastings: Tasting room is located at KLO's Farm Store, where guests can sample and purchase products. Tours in the hay wagon run Easter weekend-Oct at 11am and 1pm. Jun-Aug a 3pm tour is added. Children under 12 are free, students $3, adults $6.50. Group rate of $5 per person (min 10).

Getting There: Only 10 minutes from the centre of Kelowna, the farm is located on Dunster Road.

Highlights: Visitors can tour the working farm, which produces 4 million pounds of fruit annually. They can also visit the petting zoo, eat at the restaurant and enjoy the wonderful shopping for local arts, crafts and produce.

Wellbrook's Cranberry Orange Chutney

Featuring Wellbrook Cranberry Table Wine
and Wellbrook Fortified Cranberry Wine

Wellbrook Winery produces fruit wines, both table and dessert, from blueberries and cranberries grown by owner Terry Bremner. His Cranberry Table Wine is excellent with turkey or other poultry dishes. It has a subtle cranberry flavour and a tart finish. The Fortified Cranberry Wine is one of the most popular dessert wines and makes a great mixer for cocktails. Both the Cranberry Table Wine and Cranberry Fortified Wine were used for this delicious and nutritious cranberry chutney.

INGREDIENTS

¼ cup **Wellbrook Cranberry Table Wine**

¼ cup **Wellbrook Fortified Cranberry Wine**

2 cups granulated sugar

1 tbsp orange rind, grated

1 tbsp lemon rind, grated

¼ cup orange juice

2 tbsp lemon juice

¼ cup cider vinegar

1 tbsp ginger root, chopped

1 cinnamon stick

1½ lbs fresh cranberries

½ cup dried cranberries

1. Combine sugar, orange and lemon zests, both juices, vinegar, **Wellbrook Cranberry Table Wine**, ginger and cinnamon stick in a pot. Bring to a boil. Cook over medium-high heat, stirring constantly for 3 minutes.

2. Add fresh and dried cranberries and **Wellbrook Fortified Cranberry Wine**. Simmer, stirring occasionally, for 15 minutes or until most of the cranberries pop open. Ladle into jars and seal. Chutney will keep refrigerated for up to a month unsealed. Great on sandwiches, with chicken, turkey, pork and with salmon!

Wellbrook Winery

Location: 4626 88th Street, Delta, BC

Telephone/Fax: (604) 946-1868 / (604) 596-3624

Website: www.wellbrookwinery.com

Wine Shop, Tours and Tastings: Open for tastings daily 11am-6pm. Tours are available during the week and can be booked by phoning ahead. They focus on the history and restoration of the winery.

Getting There: Located at Highway 10 and 88th Street, 30 minutes from Vancouver and 15 minutes from Tsawwassen ferry terminal. Sign visible from Highway 99.

Highlights: You can also purchase Bremner berries and Bremner's pure berry juices. Many unique gifts and delectable food items are offered. The winery is in the 100-year-old grainery. The old barn is available for weddings and receptions.

Bonaparte Bend Wine Jelly

Featuring any of Bonaparte Bend's 12 Fruit Wine Varieties

We at Bonaparte Bend, guarantee that our wines are produced from 100% British Columbia fruit, contain the fruit on the label and contain no artificial flavourings. Top quality fruit wines are quite difficult and expensive to make. Why? Because the cost per pound for the fruit is higher than grapes and the final yield is lower. Our 12 wine varieties are apple, rhubarb, saskatoon, blackberry, boysenberry, blackcurrant, blueberry, raspberry, apricot, honey, blueberry & blackcurrant and blueberry & raspberry.

Makes 4 cups

INGREDIENTS

2 cups any **Bonaparte Bend Fruit Wine**

3 cups sugar
1 pouch liquid pectin

1. Combine **Bonaparte Bend Fruit Wine** and sugar in a medium saucepan over high heat and stir until mixture reaches a full boil.

2. Stir in liquid pectin and boil 1 minute, stirring constantly. Quickly pour into warm sterilised jars, filling to ¼ inch from the rim. Seal while hot with sterilised new lids.

Bonaparte Bend Winery

Location: 2520 Cariboo Highway, Cache Creek, BC

Telephone: (250) 457-6667

Website and Email: www.bbwinery.com, bbwines@coppervalley.bc.ca

Wine Shop, Tours and Tastings: Bistro and tasting room open Apr-Sep, Mon-Sat 10am-5pm; Sundays and Holidays 10am-4pm. Tours by appointment only and for a minimum of 20 people.

Getting There: ¼km north of Cache Creek (towards Williams Lake) on the right. About 100 feet from the highway. Easy to spot.

Highlights: Relax with a nice glass of wine and enjoy the peaceful surroundings in the country setting overlooking the Bonaparte River.

Desserts

Clearly, the pleasures wines afford are transitory – but so are those of the ballet, or of a musical performance. Wine is inspiring and adds greatly to the joy of living.

Napoleon Bonaparte 1769-1821

Mission Hill's Frozen Lemon Soufflé with Lemon Caramel Sauce

Pinot Noir Strawberry Shortcakes

Poached Okanagan Fruit

Iced Cherry Crush

Blossom's Exquisite Raspberry Chocolate Truffles

Glenugie's Baked Apples in Gamay Noir

Gewürztraminer Cake with Raspberry Sauce

Cherry Point's Blackberry Port with Fresh Berries and Vanilla Ice Cream

Summer Fruit Salad

Hainle's Fresh Fig Bouchée

Merridale's Drunken Apple-Rhubarb Aged Gouda Shortcake

Mission Hill's Frozen Lemon Soufflé with Lemon Caramel Sauce

Featuring Mission Hill Reserve Riesling Icewine

When drinking the Mission Hill 2003 Reserve Riesling Icewine luscious aromas of honeycomb, apricot and key lime will seduce your palate with its richness. Beautifully balanced by vibrant acidity, this honeyed sweetness is a rare nectar that will delight your senses. Made with 100% Riesling grapes harvested in November 2003 and January 2004. This recipe was created by winery Chef Michael Allemeier.

Serves 8–10

INGREDIENTS

½ cup **Mission Hill Reserve Riesling Icewine**

12 egg yolks

2 cups white sugar

zest from 5 lemons, finely chopped

6 egg whites

½ cup whipping cream

¼ cup water

1 cup freshly squeezed lemon juice

4 tbsp butter, cold

fresh berries for garnish

1. Prepare soufflé moulds by lining a ramekin or ring with 10cm high parchment paper, ensuring it is well secured.

2. In a large bowl add the yolks and 1¼ cups of sugar then beat until pale in colour. Cook the egg and sugar mixture over a bain marie until thickened, being careful not to overcook. Cook like a sabayon. Add chopped lemon zest and cool.

3. Whisk egg whites and ¼ cup of sugar until stiff peaks are formed. Reserve. Whip the cream with 2 tbsp of sugar.

4. Carefully fold the whipped egg white into the lemon sabayon then carefully fold in the whipped cream. Pour mixture into the prepared moulds and freeze overnight.

Mission Hill Family Estate

Location: 1730 Mission Hill Road, Westbank, BC

Telephone/Fax: (250) 768-7611 / (250) 768-2267

Website and Email: www.missionhillwinery.com, info@missionhillwinery.com

Wine Shop, Tours and Tastings: Wine shop, daily tours and tastings, culinary workshops, Estate Room tastings, seasonal Terrace Restaurant

Getting There: From Kelowna: take Highway 97 south and cross the floating bridge. Turn left onto Boucherie Road (second set of lights after Bridge Hill). Follow Boucherie approximately 5km and then turn right onto Mission Hill Road. Follow to the very top.

Highlights: Your visit includes a theatre presentation on the Okanagan Valley, a guided tour of the architecture and a visit to an underground barrel cave, described as, "easily the most dramatic cellar in Canada". Your experience will conclude with a tutored tasting of three featured wines.

Mission Hill Family Estate with the Bell Tower in the background.

5. In a clean, heavy-bottomed saucepan, mix the water and remaining sugar. Bring to a boil until the syrup starts to turn colour. Carefully add the lemon juice and reduce heat to low. Stir the syrup with a whisk until all solids have disappeared. Add butter and **Mission Hill Reserve Riesling Icewine** and whisk until butter is dissolved. Bring the sauce to a boil and remove from heat. Strain and cool.

6. If desserts are too hard, remove them from the freezer 20 minutes prior to serving. Serve with lemon caramel sauce and fresh berries. Even more delicious accompanied by a glass of **Mission Hill Reserve Riesling Icewine**.

Welcome to Mission Hill Family Estate, situated in the heart of British Columbia's breathtaking Okanagan Valley wine country, one of the Pacific Northwest's undiscovered gems.

Making great wines and providing a special place where people can enjoy them has been my dream and my life's work. Now it's a reality, one that my family and I want to share with everyone who visits us high atop Mission Hill.

We hope you'll think of our winery as a refuge from the hurried pace of daily life. We invite you to experience the nature and art of winemaking by walking our lush vineyards and visiting our underground cellars. Sample fine wines by the glass, marvel at the vista and reflect on a process that's almost as old as time itself.

We look forward to your visit.

Anthony von Mandl
Proprietor

Riesling

The Riesling grape has its origins in the Rhine and Mosel river valleys in Germany. This grape can thrive in cool climates and its resistance to frosts makes it ideally suited to Canada's unpredictable cold spells. The grape is also known as Johannesburg Riesling, Rhine Riesling or White Riesling. It is completely different from "Okanagan Riesling", which was once planted throughout the Okanagan.

Rieslings can differ in style and can be made into sweet or dry wines, although a semi-dry wine is probably the most common. In British Columbia it is sometimes used to make wonderful icewines.

The 1970s saw widespread planting of the grape in the Okanagan, where it is still very common today. Riesling is notoriously late to ripen and it is usually the last crop of the year to be harvested, as tired growers wait for the grapes to reach the desired sugar levels.

Riesling wines usually have perfumey aromas and fresh fruit flavours. Riesling is very well-suited to many types of food; it goes well with fish and seafood as well as Mexican and Asian foods. Even sushi and curry can be paired with this versatile wine.

Opposite: Blossom's Exquisite Raspberry Truffles (Pg 181)
Photo: Gary Faessler

Muller Thurgau

Ortega

Pinot Blanc

Pinot Auxerrois

Gewürztraminer

Pinot Noir

Pinot Blanc

Pinot Auxerrois

Siegerrebe

Castel

Agria

Original 1993
Experimental Planting
12 Varietals

Gewürztraminer

Zweigeltrebe

Pinot Noir

Pinot Gris

Ortega

Or

Pinot Noir Strawberry Shortcakes

Featuring BC Pinot Noir

Once upon a time, strawberries were only available once a year and then you would have to wait another 11 months before you could enjoy them again. Strawberries meant the beginning of summer; they also meant it was time for strawberry shortcakes. Nowadays we are able to enjoy this delightful dish year-round.

Serves 4

INGREDIENTS

1½ cups **BC Pinot Noir**	½ tsp salt
7 tbsp white sugar	6 tbsp butter
4 cups strawberries, hulled and halved	¾ cup milk
1 cup whipping cream	2 egg yolks
2 cups plain flour	1 tsp cornstarch
1 tbsp baking powder	1 tsp water

1. In a non-metallic bowl mix 3 tbsp sugar with **BC Pinot Noir,** stirring until the sugar dissolves. Add strawberries cover and set aside for 3 hours.

2. In a separate bowl combine 1 tbsp of sugar with cream. Whip until soft peaks form in the cream then cover and refrigerate.

3. Preheat oven to 425°F. Sift the flour, baking powder, salt and 3 tbsp of sugar into a large bowl. Using fingers or a pastry cutter, blend the butter into the dry ingredients to make a coarse, buttery mixture.

4. In a separate small bowl mix milk and egg yolks. Add the wet ingredients to the dry, mixing with a fork. Stop mixing as soon as the mixture combines to form a dough.

5. Divide the mixture into individual mounds and place them on a greased baking sheet. Bake for 15 minutes, or until shortcakes turn golden brown.

6. Remove the strawberries from the sugar and wine mixture and set both aside. In a glass, combine the cornstarch with the water and mix well. Transfer the wine mixture to a small saucepan and bring to a simmer over medium heat. Add the cornstarch mixture and stir while the wine reduces until it achieves a syrupy consistency.

7. Split each cake in half horizontally. Spread the bottom layer with butter and then cover with a layer of soaked strawberries and the Pinot Noir sauce. Cover with the top halves of the cakes and top with whipped cream and more strawberries. Drizzle with remaining sauce if desired and serve immediately.

Opposite: Ariel view of Cherry Point Vineyards in Cobble Hill
Photo courtesy of Cherry Point Vineyards

Poached Okanagan Fruit

Featuring BC Gewürztraminer

The Okanagan produces some of the best fruit in the world. Long before the wineries moved in, this whole area was full of orchards producing wonderful varieties of fruit. Today we have the best of both worlds: incredible wine and fantastic fruit. Here they are combined to make a wonderful, easy to prepare dessert.

Serves 4

INGREDIENTS

1½ cups **BC Gewürztraminer**

½ cup water

1 tsp lemon zest, chopped

1 cup sugar

1 tsp vanilla essence

1 cinnamon stick

1 large apple, cored and cubed

1 large pear, cored and cubed

1 cup fresh cherries, pitted

8 dried apricot halves, chopped

1. Over high heat in a large saucepan combine **BC Gewürztraminer**, water, lemon zest, sugar, vanilla and cinnamon. When full boil is reached add all of the fruit. Reduce heat to low and simmer for 2-3 minutes or until fruit begins to go soften.

2. Remove from the heat and let the fruit sit for 30 minutes.

3. When ready to serve, reheat fruit over low heat until just warm and serve in dessert bowls with a scoop of vanilla ice cream.

Iced Cherry Crush

Featuring BC White Wine

This is a delicious, easy to prepare dessert that will astound your friends. It is a perfect way to end a summer's day. Okanagan cherries are in season between July and August. Don't let the summer go by without trying this.

Serves 4-6

INGREDIENTS

¾ cup **BC White Wine**

½ cup honey

3 tbsp lemon juice

3 cups fresh cherries, pitted

fresh cherries for garnish

1. Combine the **BC White Wine**, honey and lemon juice in a bowl. Stir it well to make sure it is thoroughly combined.

2. Put the cherries in a food processor and pulse until they are very finely chopped.

3. Add the chopped cherries to the wine mixture and combine well. Transfer to a shallow container and place in the freezer for 40 minutes, stirring well every 10 minutes.

4. The crush mixture should be partly frozen and partly slushy when it is served. Garnish with some fresh ripe cherries.

Fruit Wine

It is possible to create wine from just about anything that contains sugar or natural starch. This means that nearly all types of fruit can be turned into wine. In British Columbia, fruit wine has become very popular, and for good reason — it is delicious.

The number of fruit wineries in British Columbia is constantly growing and many traditional wineries are now looking at adding fruit wines to their repertoire. This is because the quality of the fruit wine being produced has skyrocketed. Serious wine consumers and winemakers alike are discovering that this type of wine has a lot to offer.

One of the great things about fruit wines is that they are so easy to understand. You can be sure that a raspberry wine will taste like raspberries and a blueberry wine like blueberries. For many people this makes fruit wines easier to pair with food, for both drinking and cooking, because they are already familiar with the flavours.

If you have never tried a fruit wine, or have not tried one recently, we suggest heading out to one of the wineries and sampling some of their wares. You will be pleasantly surprised by what you find.

Blossom's Exquisite Raspberry Chocolate Truffles

Featuring Blossom Raspberry Wine

Made from raspberries in Abbotsford, this wine is the frequent winner of the popular vote at wine tasting festivals. This wine has the unmistakable sweet and tart characteristic of raspberries and is well-suited for all social occasions.

Serves 6-8

INGREDIENTS

½ cup **Blossom Raspberry Wine**

½ cup whipping cream

8 oz bittersweet chocolate

2 tbsp unsalted butter

¼ cup crushed almonds

12 oz mixed bittersweet and semisweet chocolate

2 tbsp crushed almonds (optional)

1. In a small bowl combine the **Blossom Raspberry Wine** and whipping cream and mix well. Set aside. Melt bittersweet chocolate in a double boiler or microwave. If using a microwave, stir after every 30 seconds until melted. Add raspberry cream mixture, ¼ cup crushed almonds and butter to melted chocolate and stir until thoroughly combined. Cover and place mixture in refrigerator for 4 hours, until mixture is firm.

2. Take cooled raspberry mixture and, using a teaspoon, scoop out small balls and place them on a sheet of wax paper. When all of the mixture is in balls, cover with another sheet of wax paper and return to refrigerator for 1 hour.

3. Remove balls from the refrigerator. In a double boiler or a microwave, melt mixture of bittersweet and semisweet chocolate (adjust amounts to your preference), stirring well.

4. Cover another tray with wax paper. Using 2 spoons, dip the balls one by one into the melted chocolate, covering completely, then set on waxed paper. When all truffles have been dipped, refrigerate for 2 hours. You can decorate the truffles by drizzling some more chocolate over them or sprinkling them with crushed almonds. These delicious chocolates can be stored in an airtight container for weeks and are heavenly served with a glass of **Blossom Raspberry Wine**.

Blossom Winery

Location: 5491 Minoru Boulevard, Richmond, BC

Telephone/Fax: (604) 232-9839 / (604) 232-9836

Website and Email: www.blossomwinery.com, info@blossomwinery.com

Wine Shop, Tours and Tastings: Free tasting at the winery. Open Mon-Fri 10am-6pm and Sat 11am-6pm. For tours please call to make an appointment.

Getting There: Close to Vancouver, the winery is located just off the Westminster Highway on Minoru Boulevard in Richmond.

Highlights: Blossom Winery produces a unique and dynamic selection of wines to excite every palate and compliment every portfolio. Their creations include the delectable Raspberry Wine, Passion Fruit Wine and a variety of premium-grade reds and whites befitting any dining occasion.

Glenugie's Baked Apples in Gamay Noir

Featuring Glenugie Winery Gamay Noir

The 2002 Gamay Noir has a beautiful garnet colour and a lightly oaked nose with blueberries and blackberries to follow. It has a lively and complex taste with a long, lingering finish. In this recipe the Gamay Noir is turned into a sauce after baking. It is very important to use an apple variety that holds its shape or the apples will collapse.

Serves 4

INGREDIENTS

1 cup **Glenugie Winery Gamay Noir**

¼ cup dried cranberries

¼ cup pitted dates

¼ cup chopped almonds

2 tbsp butter

4 apples (Golden Delicious or Mutsu work very well)

½ cup cranberry juice

½ cup granulated sugar

1. Preheat oven to 375°F. Combine cranberries, dates, almonds and butter in a food processor. Purée until pasty.

2. Peel the top third of the apple. Core the apple to make enough space for the filling but leave a little apple at the base. Divide the purée mixture into 4 parts and stuff into the apples.

3. Combine **Glenugie Winery Gamay Noir**, cranberry juice and sugar in a baking dish. Add the apples and bake for 50-60 minutes, or until apples are tender when pierced with a toothpick. Baste occasionally with the sauce.

4. Pour the sauce into a pot. Bring to a boil and reduce until slightly thickened, 7-8 minutes. Place the apples on 4 plates and top with the sauce.

Glenugie Winery

Location: 3033 232nd Street, Langley, BC

Telephone / Fax: (604) 539-9463, 1 (866) 233-9463 / (604) 539-9464

Website and Email: www.glenugiewinery.com, info@glenugiewinery.com

Wine Shop, Tours and Tastings: Wine shop and tasting room open Sun-Wed noon-6pm and Thu-Sat 11am-6pm. Tours May-Aug at 1pm and 3pm. Private tours available by appointment.

Getting There: Via Highway 1, take exit 66 to 232nd Street. Via Highway 99 take the 8th Avenue exit to 16th Avenue and head east. Located in South Langley between 16th Avenue and Fraser Highway.

Highlights: A family-owned and operated, organically-grown vineyard with a new state-of-the-art winery facility. Try the award-winning wines grown from 100% BC-grown grapes and discover the Scottish history behind the name Glenugie.

Gewürztraminer Cake with Raspberry Sauce

Featuring BC Gewürztraminer

Wine in a cake?! Absolutely! This cake also works very well with Riesling. Try it and you will not regret it.

Serves 6

INGREDIENTS

1 cup **BC Gewürztraminer**

4 eggs, whites and yolks separated

1¼ cups sugar

1½ tsp vanilla extract

²/₃ cup vegetable oil

2 cups flour, sifted

1 tbsp baking powder

¼ tsp of salt

2 lbs fresh raspberries

sugar to taste

whipped cream

1. Preheat oven to 350°F. In a bowl beat the egg yolks with the vanilla and half of the sugar. Add the **BC Gewürztraminer** and oil and continue to beat. Carefully fold in the flour and baking powder.

2. In a separate bowl beat the egg whites with the salt until soft peaks are formed. Add the remaining sugar and continue to beat until stiff peaks are formed. Gently fold the stiff egg whites into the wine and flour mixture.

3. Prepare a greased loaf pan approximately 16 inches by 5 inches and pour the mixture into it. Bake in the oven for 45 minutes.

4. Meanwhile, purée the berries in a blender or food processor. If the purée is not sweet enough add sugar to taste.

5. Create a pool of purée on the plate and lay 2 slices of cake on top. Serve with whipped cream.

Gewürztraminer

Pronounced (gaa-verts-tra-mee-ner)

Wine historians disagree on the meaning and origins of the word Gewürztraminer. However, most report that the name comes from the word "gewurz", a German word meaning spicy and the word "Traminer", which is a variety of grape.

Traminer comes from the Italian village of Termeno located in Germany's Tyrolean Alps. The grape had been growing very successfully there since the Middle Ages. Sometime in the last few hundred years the grape mutated into the grape we know today as Gewürztraminer. Today the grape is commonly grown in the Alsace region of France.

The grape grows in British Columbia with much success. It is a variety with distinct aromatic characteristics of flowers and spicy perfumes, similar to Muscat. The wine can be stored for a few years without problems but is best consumed young.

Gewürztraminer is a great accompaniment for a wide variety of foods including spicy foods, stone fruits, game, poultry and cheese boards.

Cherry Point's Blackberry Port with Fresh Berries and Vanilla Ice Cream

Featuring Cowichan Blackberry Port

A heady aroma of sweet blackberry fruit is followed by a warm, velvety mouth feel with smoky, aromatic and intense blackberry fruit. Spicy black fruit lingers on the long finish. Delicious on its own, it is also divine with desserts, dark chocolate, figs and ice cream. This recipe proves that the simple things in life are often the best.

Serves 4

INGREDIENTS

½ cup **Cowichan Blackberry Port**   4 cups fresh berries

8 scoops rich French vanilla ice cream

1. Layout 4 bowls and place 2 scoops of ice cream into each. While ice cream is still hard, drizzle 1 ounce of **Cowichan Blackberry Port** over the top of each serving, followed by a cup of fresh berries.

2. Serve immediately with a glass of **Cowichan Blackberry Port**. See, we told you it would be simple.

Cherry Point Vineyards

Location: 840 Cherry Point Road, Cobble Hill, BC

Telephone/Fax: (250) 743-1272 / (250) 743-1059

Website and Email: www.cherrypointvineyards.com, info@cherrypointvineyards.com

Wine Shop, Tours and Tastings: Open every day throughout the year for select wine tastings. Tours at 1pm every Sat and Sun.

Getting There: Located 40 minutes north of Victoria. Watch for the "Wine Route" signs. Travel along Fisher Road, connecting to Telegraph Road. Turn right at Cherry Point Road.

Highlights: Visit our wine shop for unique wine. Our patio is open every summer.

Summer Fruit Salad

Featuring BC Riesling

This recipe uses honeydew melon, grapes, blueberries and strawberries, but - as with any fruit salad - the possibilities are endless. Use whatever fresh fruit you have access to: berries, apples, pears and pineapple would all be wonderful thrown into this summer treat.

Serves 4

INGREDIENTS

1 cup **BC Riesling**

¼ cup sugar

½ large honeydew melon, cubed

1 cup blueberries

1½ cups seedless grapes, halved lengthways

10 oz fresh strawberries, quartered

1 tbsp fresh mint, chopped

1. In a small saucepan combine the **BC Riesling** and sugar. Bring it to a boil and stir until the sugar dissolves. Let it simmer for 2 minutes before removing it from the heat.

2. Combine the fruit and mint in a bowl and pour the warm wine mixture over the top. Mix thoroughly, cover and refrigerate for 2 hours, stirring occasionally. Only serve when it has been thoroughly chilled.

Hainle's Fresh Fig Bouchée

Featuring Hainle Vineyards Zweigelt

This mouth-filling, smooth and fruit forward red has enjoyed good popularity with consumers and judges alike. Raspberry, blackberry, currant and cocoa notes dominate the aromas. It matches wonderfully with pork, poultry, seafood and desserts.

Serves 4

INGREDIENTS

1 cup **Hainle Vineyards Zweigelt**

1 vanilla pod

¾ cup granulated sugar

$1^1/_3$ cups all-purpose flour

¼ tsp salt

½ cup cold unsalted butter, cubed

1 large egg yolk

1½ tbsp water

spray cooking oil

6 large fresh figs

1 fresh lemon

1 cup mascarpone

icing sugar to garnish

1. Split vanilla pod lengthways with a knife and remove the meat from the pod. Combine the pod and the meat with the **Hainle Vineyards Zweigelt** and ½ cup sugar in a small saucepan. Simmer until you have syrup. Remove from heat and set aside to thicken. Set the vanilla pod aside to use later as a garnish.

2. Mix flour, remaining sugar and salt in a large bowl. Blend in butter with fingers or a pastry cutter until it resembles coarse meal with small butter lumps. In a separate bowl beat together yolk and water, then add to flour mixture and stir well. Gently knead mixture with floured hands, just until dough forms. Turn out dough onto a floured surface and knead gently 4-5 more times. Form into a ball then flatten into a 5-inch disk. Wrap in saran wrap and chill for 1 hour.

3. Preheat oven to 325°F. Roll out sweet pastry, making small disks about 4-5mm thick. Spray the back of large muffin tins and lay disks over the backs, poking small holes through the bottom of the pastry so it doesn't rise. Place in oven and bake until pastry cups have light brown edges. Remove and cool.

4. Cut figs into quarters and squeeze lemon juice over them. Heat sauce and drizzle on serving plate around pastry cups. Spoon mascarpone into pastry cup and top with the figs. Garnish with a spear of vanilla pod. Dust with icing sugar.

Hainle Vineyards & Deep Creek Wine Estate

Location: 5355 Trepanier Bench Road, Peachland, BC

Telephone/Fax: (250) 767-2525, 1 (800) 767-3109 / (250) 767-2543

Website and Email: www.hainle.com, info@hainle.com

Wine Shop, Tours and Tastings: Join us for tours, tastings and shopping 7 days a week. Enjoy Chef Derek Thompson's fine cuisine in the Amphora Bistro or bring your picnic basket and enjoy the view of the lake.

Getting There: A short distance down Trepanier Bench Road, just north of Peachland.

Highlights: International organic standards govern the vineyard. Learn how organic wines and conventional wines differ.

Zweigelt

PRONOUNCED (TSVI-GELT)

IN AUSTRIA, DURING THE EARLY 1920S, DR FRITZ ZWEIGELT CROSSED THE BLAUFRÄNKISH AND SAINT LAURENT VARIETIES OF GRAPE AND CAME UP WITH SOMETHING NEW. THAT NEW VARIETY BECAME KNOWN AS ZWEIGELT.

TODAY THIS IS THE MOST COMMONLY GROWN RED WINE GRAPE IN AUSTRIA. AUSTRIA HAS A LONG HISTORY OF WINEMAKING AND ARCHAEOLOGICAL EVIDENCE SUGGESTS THAT WINE HAS BEEN PRODUCED THERE AS EARLY AS 700 BC.

THE WINE IS A NEWCOMER TO BRITISH COLUMBIA AND IT MADE ITS FIRST APPEARANCE HERE AROUND THE TURN OF THE MILLENNIUM. IT HAS SINCE BECOME VERY POPULAR. A GREAT WINE IN ITS OWN RIGHT, ZWEIGELT CAN ALSO BE BLENDED WITH OUTSTANDING RESULTS.

ZWEIGELT IS BEST CONSUMED WHEN IT IS RELATIVELY YOUNG AND FRESH, ALTHOUGH IT CAN BE CELLARED FOR A FEW YEARS WITHOUT ANY PROBLEMS. AUSTRIANS SWEAR THAT THE WINE IS PERFECT WITH WIENER SCHNITZEL. IT CAN ALSO BE PAIRED SUCCESSFULLY WITH SEAFOOD AND BOTH WHITE AND RED MEATS, SUCH AS GRILLED CHICKEN, RIBS, LAMB AND ROAST PORK.

Merridale's Drunken Apple-Rhubarb Aged Gouda Shortcake

Featuring Merridale Winter Apple Cider

Winter Apple Cider is a fresh and velvety sipping drink with an aroma of baked apples and buttery brown sugar. It can be served straight, in the tradition of port, or paired with cheddar, blue cheese, melons, fruit desserts and dark chocolate. La Pommeraie Chef John Waller created this recipe especially for this book.

Serves 4-6

INGREDIENTS

6 tbsp **Merridale Winter Apple Cider**	2 eggs
1½ cups whipping cream	½ cup light cream
½ cup cold butter, cubed + 2 tbsp	½ cup aged Gouda or sharp aged
2 cups all-purpose flour	cheddar, grated
3 tbsp baking powder	2 cups rhubarb, cut in ½ inch chunks
1 cup sugar	2 large Braeburn apples, finely diced

1. Combine whipping cream, 3 tbsp **Merridale Winter Apple Cider** and 2 tbsp butter in a saucepan over medium heat and reduce by two-thirds. Cool in refrigerator for 2 hours or overnight.

2. Preheat oven to 350°F. Sift together flour, baking powder and ½ cup of sugar. Blend in butter with a pastry cutter or with your fingers, distributing the butter evenly. In a separate bowl beat eggs then add light cream. Add the wet to the dry ingredients, add the cheese and GENTLY mix together with a fork.

3. Turn the mixture out on a lightly floured surface and GENTLY form a disk about 7 inches in diameter and ½ inch thick. Cut the disk into quarters or sixths. Bake on a greased baking sheet for 20 minutes or until golden brown.

4. In a saucepan combine rhubarb, remaining sugar, 2 tbsp **Merridale Winter Apple Cider** and cook until rhubarb is soft. Add apple and remaining cider. Stir well and remove from heat. Cut the shortcake in half and spoon the apple rhubarb mixture on top with a healthy dollop of clotted cream. Serve with a glass of **Merridale Winter Apple Cider**.

Merridale Ciderworks

Location: 1230 Merridale Road, Cobble Hill, BC

Telephone/Fax: (250) 743-4293, 1 (800) 998-9908 / (250) 743-9310

Website and Email: www.merridalecider.com, info@merridalecider.com

Wine Shop, Tours and Tastings: Take a self-guided tour and learn about cider making. Enjoy a free tasting in the Cider House. La Pommeraie restaurant is nestled in the heart of the orchard and is open daily 11am-3pm and Fri-Sat 5pm-9pm.

Getting There: 40 minutes from Victoria. Turn off the highway onto Shawnigan-Mill Bay Road. Turn right onto Cameron Taggert Road. Turn right on Merridale Road.

Highlights: Visit for the Summer Solstice July 17-19, Harvest Wine Celebration Oct 1-2 and Christmas Magic during the month of December.

Drinks

What contemptible scoundrel stole the cork from my lunch?

W. C. Fields 1880-1946

Mulled Wine

Raspberry Mimosa

Sangria

White Wine Sangria

The Paradise Martini

Peaches & Riesling

The Apple Attack

Merlot Magic

The Perfect Caesar

Summer Citrus Spritzer

Mulled Wine

Featuring BC Red Wine

Mulled wine was known as Ypocras or Hipocris during the Middle Ages, named after the ancient physician Hippocrates. Today mulled wine is often served on the ski slopes or at Christmas festivities. It is a great treat to come home to after a harsh winter's day. There are many variations to this recipe but we like this basic old-fashioned version.

Makes approximately 10 glasses

INGREDIENTS

2 bottles **BC Red Wine**

1 large orange

1 large lemon

½ cup water

½ cup sugar

5 sticks cinnamon

4 whole cloves

1. Remove the zest from the fruit, leaving the white pith. Set the fruit aside. Combine the zest with the water, sugar, cinnamon and cloves in a large saucepan over medium heat. Bring to a boil and then simmer for 5 minutes.

2. Slice the lemon and orange. Add the **BC Red Wine** and fruit to the mixture on the stovetop. Be very careful not to boil the wine. The saying for mulled wine goes "if it boils, it spoils". It should take about 30-40 minutes to heat thoroughly over low heat.

3. Strain the mixture and serve. Leftover wine can be saved and heated on a low heat in the microwave the next day.

Opposite: The Sonora Room at Night
Photo courtesy of Burrowing Owl Estate Winery

Raspberry Mimosa

Featuring BC Sparkling Wine and BC Raspberry Wine

Champagne and orange juice make up the mimosa and here we give it a little extra something by adding the taste of raspberries. Another alternative to this drink is to leave out the orange juice, throw in a couple of fresh raspberries and "voila": you have a Raspberry Kir Royale!

Serves 1

INGREDIENTS

2 oz **BC Sparkling Wine**

2 oz orange juice

½ oz **BC Raspberry Wine** (or Chambord)

1. In a champagne flute start by pouring the orange juice, then top with the **BC Sparkling Wine**. The sparkling wine will make its way down through the orange juice, filling it with wonderful bubbles. Finally, top it off with **BC Raspberry Wine**. Do not stir or you will lose some of your precious bubbles!

Opposite: Inniskillin Okanagan Vineyards' winemaker, Sandor Mayer, just prior to the 2004 icewine harvest.
Photo: Brian Sprout courtesy of Vincor

Sparkling Wine

"It's like drinking the stars!" exclaimed Dom Perignon, the Benedictine monk as he sipped on a glass of champagne. Champagne is in fact a region in France where sparkling wine achieved worldwide fame. All wine that undergoes a second fermentation, carbonation, is called sparkling wine. International law forbids any other wine region from using the term "champagne" to label sparkling wine, although in Canada many wineries use the same methods as those employed in France to make the bubbly beverage.

Other countries have created their own regional names to distinguish their versions of this festive drink. It is called "Cava" in Spain, "Spumante" in Italy and "Sekt" in Germany and Austria. In the United States some sparkling wines are still labelled "champagne" due to a complex legal loophole. The US never ratified the Treaty of Versailles after World War I, part of which covered the naming of wines after regions. Therefore these producers argue that they are not obliged to adhere to these laws.

In British Columbia we have a wonderful variety of high-quality sparkling wines available at all price ranges. Sparkling wine should be served chilled. This can be done quickly by placing the bottle in a sink full of ice and water. When opening a bottle of sparkling wine, carefully remove the foil cage, being sure not to point the bottle at anyone. Then grip the cork firmly, and gently turn the bottle, easing the cork free.

The aroma should be clean and fresh and citrus notes in the wine are usually a good sign. The smaller the bubbles the better, as they dance in the mouth creating a creamy sensation, as opposed to the "soda water fizz" created by large bubbles.

Sparkling wine is usually only consumed on special occasions, but this need not be the case as it pairs well with most types of food. It is especially wonderful at breakfast and it is well worth investing in a sparkling wine sealer so that you can save some of the previous night's bottle especially for this reason.

Sangria

Featuring BC Red Wine

Sangria originates from a traditional red wine punch that has been in Europe for hundreds of years. Originally the base would have been a red wine from Bordeaux. Later it was made in Spain with Rioja. There are no limits to what you can do and it is fun to experiment with this recipe, using your favourite reds, fruits and spirits to create your own masterpiece.

Serves 10

INGREDIENTS

1 bottle **BC Red Wine**	4 oz white rum
1 lemon	1 oz triple sec
1 lime	2 oz raw sugar
2 oranges	1 oz fresh lemon juice
2 apples	8 oz fresh orange juice
4 oz brandy	16 oz club soda

1. Slice the apple into pieces and the citrus fruit into wheels, removing the seeds. Mix brandy, triple sec, rum and sugar in a large bowl and soak the fruit overnight in the mixture.

2. The next morning add the **BC Red Wine** and fruit juice to the mixture and refrigerate until it is time to serve.

3. Just before serving add the club soda to the bowl and gently stir. Scoop out some fruit from the punch bowl placing a little in the bottom of each glass. Top with ice and then fill with sangria for a wonderfully refreshing summer treat.

White Wine Sangria

Featuring BC White Wine

Here is a version of sangria using white wine. The fruits in this version make a very pretty drink and it tastes fabulous as well. Like always, change the fruits around to use whatever is available. Half the fun of making sangria is experimenting – as long as the ingredients are fresh, the wine is good and you do not go overboard on the sugar or spirits, it will taste great.

Makes 8 glasses

INGREDIENTS

1 bottle **BC White Wine**, chilled

½ lb watermelon, cubed or scooped out as balls

1 orange, halved, sliced and seeded

1 lime, sliced and seeded

¼ cantaloupe, cubed

2 kiwi fruits, peeled and sliced

1 cup seedless green grapes

1 cup seedless red grapes

1 tbsp sugar

½ cup triple sec

½ cup brandy

1 cup white cranberry juice, chilled

1. Combine all of the fruit in a large pitcher.

2. In a separate bowl combine the sugar, brandy and triple sec. Stir well, trying to dissolve as much of the sugar as possible.

3. Add the sugar and spirits mixture to the fruit and let it sit for 1 hour, giving it a stir every 15 minutes and coating as much fruit as possible.

4. Add the **BC White Wine** and the white cranberry juice and serve chilled.

The Paradise Martini

Featuring Paradise Ranch VQA Icewine and Late Harvest Wine

Paradise Ranch Wines offers Chardonnay, Merlot and Riesling varietals. All of our wines make decadent martinis and can be used in the traditional style of icewine combined with vodka or gin, or can be matched with the fruit juice of your choice. Citrus blends go best with red wines and cranberry with white wines. Add a splash of club soda to add some sparkle!

Makes as many martinis as you can create!

INGREDIENTS

1 part **Paradise Ranch Late Harvest**
Wine or Icewine

1 part vodka or gin

½ part juice of your choice

½ part club soda

1 bunch frozen grapes for garnish

1. Combine **Paradise Ranch Late Harvest Wine** or **Icewine**, spirits and fruit juice, shake over ice and strain into chilled cocktail glasses.

2. Add club soda and garnish with frozen grapes!

Paradise Ranch Wines Corp.

Telephone/Fax: (604) 683-6040 / (604) 683-8611

Website and Email: www.icewines.com, info@icewines.com

Highlights: These dessert wine specialists produce internationally acclaimed wines. Recent vintages of the fine icewines and late harvest wines have won over 70 prestigious awards. The innovative bottle design, with a window looking through to an illustration of a grizzly bear feasting on vineyard grapes, has also been awarded with many international accolades.

Where to Buy: In British Columbia the wines are available at VQA wine shops, provincial government liquor stores and at many private wine shops and cold beer & wine stores. Also available in over 25 states in the Unites States and more than 10 countries. Please email for full details.

Peaches & Riesling

Featuring BC Riesling

Everybody knows about peaches and cream; that is old hat. Here we have a peaches and Riesling recipe that makes a wine cooler that will satisfy your summer thirst. A perfect welcome drink for guests this is also a great treat after any strenuous physical activity.

Serves 6

INGREDIENTS

1 bottle **BC Riesling**

1 can of peaches in syrup (15 oz)

½ cup triple sec

½ cup fresh orange juice

¼ cup sugar

1 orange, halved and sliced

1. Combine the **BC Riesling** with the peaches, syrup, triple sec, orange juice and sugar in a large pitcher and mix well.

2. Add the orange slices to the pitcher. Cover and place in the refrigerator for 2 hours or until it is well chilled.

3.Serve chilled in large wine glasses.

The Apple Attack

Featuring BC Chardonnay

Mixologist Gavin Forbes has worked in around 50 of the world's finest cocktail bars and has become a living bartending institution. For Cooking with BC Wine he has created two unusual, yet outstanding martinis that use BC wine as a base.

Serves 1

INGREDIENTS

1½ oz **BC Chardonnay**

1 oz green apple puree

1½ oz vodka (Zubrowka if possible)

¾ oz apple liqueur

1. Combine all of the ingredients in a cocktail shaker with ice. Stir well and then strain into a chilled martini glass.

2. Cheers.

Merlot Magic

Featuring BC Merlot

A mixologist is a person who practices the art of making exceptional cocktails. Different methods can be employed including, blending, shaking, stirring, muddling and layering. A mixologist must explore and extend the boundaries of possibility, focusing on the taste and appearance of the drinks they create. Cocktail maestro Gavin Forbes created this masterpiece. Prepare to have your taste buds tantalised; you have never tasted anything like this!

Serves 2

INGREDIENTS

3 oz **BC Merlot**

3 oz raspberry vodka

1½ oz raspberry purée

1½ oz Chambord (raspberry liqueur)

1 oz condensed milk

dash of vanilla sugar

red grapes for garnish

1. Combine all of the liquid ingredients in a cocktail shaker with ice. Add the vanilla sugar. Shake well and then strain into chilled martini glasses and garnish with red grapes.

2 Congratulations, you are now well on your way to becoming a certified mixologist.

Vanilla Sugar

Vanilla sugar is a fragrant and flavourful addition to your pantry. Thankfully it is also very easy to make.

All you need are vanilla beans, an airtight container and sugar. Cut your vanilla beans into 1½ inch pieces, using two beans for every pound of sugar. Fill the container halfway with sugar and then drop in the vanilla beans. Top the container with sugar and seal. Store the sugar for 3 weeks before removing the vanilla beans. Some people swear that keeping the container in a dark place makes the sugar taste even better. Vanilla beans can be reused for this purpose for 6 months to a year.

Vanilla sugar is great on baked goods, on fruit, in desserts and of course in cocktails. It also makes a wonderful gift and is a fabulous addition to hampers.

The Perfect Caesar

Featuring BC Red Wine

The Caesar was invented in 1969 by Mr. Walter Chell to celebrate the opening of Marco's restaurant in Calgary, Alberta. The original recipe does not actually call for red wine, but we feel it makes the drink much better because anything tomato-based is improved with wine.

Serves 1

INGREDIENTS

1 dash **BC Red Wine**

2 oz vodka

6 oz Clamato juice

1 pinch celery salt

3 drops Worcestershire sauce

2 drops Tabasco sauce (or to taste)

1 wedge of fresh lime

pepper to taste

1 pickled bean or asparagus stalk for garnish

celery salt for the rim

1. Rub the wedge of lime around the rim of a highball glass. Holding the glass upside down, dip it in a pile of celery salt to coat the rim. Fill the glass with ice.

2 Add all the ingredients listed above except the garnish. Stir well and garnish with a pickled bean or asparagus.

3. Make another one!

Summer Citrus Spritzer

Featuring BC White Wine

The word "spritzer" comes from the German word "spritzig" meaning fizzy, bubbly and lively. That is a great way to describe this summer refreshment which is immensely popular throughout the world. This drink is so popular in Romania that winemakers there actually make their white wines specifically with the spritzer in mind.

Serves 1

INGREDIENTS

2 parts **BC White Wine**

1 part citrus soda water

1 slice of lemon

1 slice of lime

1. Okay, this seems very simple and it is. Fill glasses with ice, slide the fruit slices down between the ice and the inside of the glass. Add the **BC White Wine** and top with the citrus soda water. To make a regular spritzer just use regular soda water and you can omit the fruit, if you prefer.

Index

SPECIAL THANKS

A special thanks to everyone who went out of their way to help us put this book together. It would not have been possible without your time, advice and generosity. Of special note are Gary Faessler, Michael Strang, Cassandra Whalen and all of the hard-working winery owners and winemakers of British Columbia. Thank you to the "Tuscan Kitchen" in Victoria and "Pots and Paraphernalia" in Duncan for allowing us to use their beautiful tableware for the photographs. And thank you to our parents for their inspiration, enthusiasm and encouragement.

FURTHER READING

For further reading on the wineries and wines of British Columbia we recommend trying one of John Schreiner's books. Having written several books on the British Columbia wine region and industry, John Schreiner is recognised as the foremost expert on this topic. His work was a great help to us in our research for this book. Recent titles by John Schreiner include *The Wineries of British Columbia* and *British Columbia Wine Country*.

SCENIC PHOTOGRAPHY

When compiling the scenic photography for this book we approached numerous wineries and asked for their best shots. Time and time again we were given photographs taken by photographer Brian Sprout. More of Brian's work can be viewed at www.briansprout.com.

ABOUT THE AUTHORS

Photo Jim Perceval

Troy Townsin was born in Melbourne, Australia and worked as an actor and playwright before embarking on a round-the-world backpacking extravaganza. After his return to Melbourne he earned a Bachelor of Arts in International Studies, taking semesters in Malaysia, Turkey and the UK. While studying in Malaysia he met his future wife Cheryl-Lynn. After graduating, he worked for the United Nations Information Centre in London before taking a job as an event reporter. In 2003, he won the prestigious Travel Writer of the Year award with TNT Magazine UK. Troy is proud to be a resident of British Columbia and his backpack is now hanging in his home in Victoria, BC

Cheryl-Lynn Townsin was born and raised in British Columbia. She completed her Bachelor of Commerce in International Business at the University of Victoria. Pursuing an international career in business she has worked and travelled extensively throughout South East Asia, Europe and the Middle East. Eventually the lure of British Columbia proved too much and she returned to her motherland and has now settled in Victoria, BC.

ABOUT THE PHOTOGRAPHER/CONTRIBUTOR

Gary Faessler is a food and wine writer/photographer based in Duncan, BC. Gary produced and hosted "Chefs about Town" British Columbia's first regional culinary arts television series broadcast across Canada. He has been published in four cookbooks and has written numerous articles for Vancouver Magazine, Northwest Palate and Vancouver Lifestyles Magazine.